Social Media Made Simple

How to Avoid Social Media Suicide

4th Edition

Concise Training

By Mary Thomas

Alison.

Happy Reading!.

Mary Thomas.

Fourth Edition published 2015
Copyright ©Mary Thomas 2015
Appletree Publications
Coombe Road
Compton
Berkshire RG20 6RQ

Call: 01635 578 500

Email: Books@Appletreeuk.com

Website: www.Appletreeuk.com

These materials have been developed by Mary Thomas and all the content and the accuracy are the sole responsibility of Mary Thomas.

ISBN 978-0-9570913-1-3

Cover, design and typesetting by Clockwork Graphic Design

Contents

Social Media is no longer a buzz phrase; it has become part of everyday communication used by celebrities, broadcast media as well as business. But what is social media and what is the best way to use it for business? How can it be used so that it doesn't take up too much time and resources with few real, measurable results? Has it moved on from people talking about what they had for breakfast?

During the past seven years of providing social media marketing training and consultancy to small and medium sized business, I have seen businesses who have dabbled in Social Media with little real success, as well as businesses who have embraced the available channels with a clear idea of how to go forward. The latter have seen direct success and money added to their bottom line as a result.

To me, Social Media is one method of marketing. I believe it to be the most cost effective and time efficient way of marketing today – but only if done properly. I believe Social Media is made up of a number of channels – you just need to pick the right channels for the job you need to do.

This book was born out of watching business owners attending free talks and presentations on Social Media and hearing that they needed to join in or get left behind. These businesses registered with a number of Social Networking sites – Twitter, Facebook and LinkedIn, added relevant links to their website and updated their status for a week or too – and lost interest.

Let me give you a scenario:

You are interested in working with Company A because you have met an employee or the company has been recommended. You have a look at the website of Company A and notice they have a link to Twitter. You would like to find out more about Company A, so you click through to see what they are saying. You find that Company A has six followers and two tweets.

What impression does this give you about Company A?

What do you think? Is it better to have no Twitter profile than one that was started and then abandoned?

In my opinion, if you are going to start using Social Media channels, you need to keep going. This has a number of implications in terms of time and cost of resource. Yes, many Social Media channels are free – you don't need to pay to register on Social Networking sites or to upload YouTube videos. You can even start a blog for free, but don't underestimate the cost in terms of resource. You will need to have the time to use the channels, to listen to others, plan what you are going to say, and actually say it.

This can be quite an issue for many small and medium sized businesses, but don't despair, not all Social Media channels are right for every business. There are many factors to take into account.

This workbook will help you. We will explain the issues you need to think about and then we provide worksheets to implement what you have learnt. If you work through the book and take the time to think through and fill in the worksheets, you will end up with a Social Media Strategy and a plan for implementation going forward.

So what do we cover in this book?

In Chapter 1, we look at what we mean by Social Media and how this powerful form of marketing has developed over the past nine or so years.

We also consider what we mean by the term 'Strategy' and the elements that need to be considered when identifying a strategy to use to go forward.

In Chapter 2, we look at the first element of creating a Strategy – Review. Before we start to look at Social Media Marketing we need to think about what, if anything, you are currently doing to market your business. We want to look at how much this is costing you in terms of time and money and what 'success' (whatever that means) you are achieving. It is unlikely that Social Media will completely replace your traditional marketing so we need to identify how you can divert your limited resources. We ask you to examine the quality of your current marketing materials and how they reflect your brand and values.

Next, we look at why are you are bothering with Social Media. You will, I'm sure, have identified certain objectives for your business as part of your business plan. Ultimately you will have the overall objective of making a profit, but how can you use Social Media to help you achieve this? What are your aims for your Social Media?

In Chapter 4 we look at who you are going to talk to using the Social Media channels. Who is your audience and where are they going to be on Social Media? Your audience will be made up of a number of different groups and will be your customers, as well as suppliers, peers and people who can influence what others think of your business. We will help you to look at each of the groups you want to engage with and how this impacts which Social Media channels you use and what you say.

In Chapter 5 we consider 'keywords' and why it is important you understand your keywords for your website as well as your Social Media.

At this stage in the book, we will be in a position to look in more detail at Social Media marketing. I believe that Social Media marketing can be done using a number of channels – each with their own strengths and weaknesses and each applicable to a different type of business. We give an overview of the main characteristics of each channel and give examples of how businesses we know, like you, are using them. We look at the resource requirements for each channel and give you some suggestions for how you might measure success. For each channel, we encourage you to think about whether it will apply to your business now and in the medium and long term.

Having identified a set of potential channels, we use Chapter 7 to do a reality check in terms of the resources you have available. We will discuss the pros and cons of outsourcing your Social Media, keeping it in-house or using a combination of methods. If you are a sole trader you are unlikely to be able to use all of the Social Media channels well. If you try, you may not get any paid work done! We need to revisit the potential channels you selected in Chapter 6 and think about the time, skills and money you have available. If you are using internal resources, you need to be aware of and plan for any training needs, or creation of policy guidelines for employees.

A key part of a Social Media marketing strategy is planning what you are going to say using each of the channels. In Chapter 8, we give you some ideas of the type of messages you can deliver using each of the channels; and encourage you to create a content calendar for your business.

It is important that your use of Social Media is measured against targets. In Chapter 9, we help you to understand how you are going to measure the success of each of your aims. Indeed what do you mean by the term 'success'? We also cover how to measure the return on investment of Social Media and indicate some ways you can do this. Without this information, how are you going to know whether what you are doing is working?

Taking all these points into consideration, we will now be ready to create your Social Media Strategy. You will need to consider a Strategy for you as an individual and if appropriate, your employees, as well as for your business. Once you have created your Strategy, you have to create your implementation plan and understand how to use each of the channels. You may need some training before this can happen.

You are still not finished though, because Social Media is changing and developing so rapidly that I would recommend you have a look at your Strategy every six months. You may find you need to start again at Review in Chapter 2!

For now, let's get started with Chapter 1 and look at what Social Media actually is.

CHAPTER ONE

1.1 Some History

The World Wide Web (WWW) was created in 1989 by CERN physicist Tim Berners-Lee. On 30 April 1993, CERN announced that the World Wide Web would be "freely usable by anyone". Combined with the development of computers becoming cheaper and smaller, the new technology age was well and truly upon us. Email became commonplace and it became usual for a business to have a website.

In 2004, Tim O'Reilly talked about Web 2.0 as a way of building applications on the internet rather than on desktop computers. Products were built and accessed by a group of people. This led to people using tools on the internet to communicate with each other.

In 2006, Time Magazine selected the 'Person of The Year' as the public who were participating in content creation on social networks, blogs, wikis and media sharing sites .

As I write this we are at the end of 2015 and the use of Web 2.0 has developed to be more than "a massive social experiment" (Times Magazine, 2006) and is used by celebrities and businesses throughout the world to communicate with their fans and customers. Twitter, LinkedIn and Facebook have become incorporated companies and even part of our everyday language. Over half the time people in the UK spend on the Internet (89% of the population) is spent on social media. (Fleischmann, 2015). But what do we mean by the term 'Social Media'?

1.2 What is Social Media?

Social Media is the term used to describe the various activities that are used by businesses, consumers, celebrities and others to communicate on the internet. I define Social Media as:

"A way of engaging with a large number of people in a cost effective, time efficient way."

The key word here is "engaging". Why should businesses engage? There are a number of reasons including:

1 Customer Service and Awareness

Before the use of Social Media, people would talk to their small groups of friends in the pub or in other social occasions, about the service or product that they had recently experienced. Comments would be directed to a small group of people and probably quite informally and infrequently. Social Media allows people to comment easily and immediately (particularly through the use of Mobile devices), to a large number of people – many of whom may not be known well or personally. These comments are normally available in the public arena of the internet.

It is absolutely true that there is still a large number of people who don't want to be involved in Social Media, but can you afford not to know if somebody talks about the bad (or good) service they had with your business?

For Example

In 2010, I stayed in a Hilton Hotel, just off the motorway. I was charged for parking in addition to the bed & breakfast rate, but I would have struggled to get to the hotel without a car. I felt that it would have been better to have one inclusive rate.

The next day, I wrote on Twitter: "I was surprised to have been charged extra for parking at the Hilton last night".

This was seen by (at the time) 2,000 of my followers. Two of these followers picked up on this comment and forwarded it to their followers. Within minutes, the comment had been seen by approximately 10,000 people worldwide! Hilton Hotels didn't respond. Were they listening?

I wasn't trying to cause trouble or be particularly negative, but by their apparent lack of interest, they have lost a customer.

It would have been very easy, if Hilton Hotels had been listening, for them to respond to the comment with a positive spin or explanation.

2 Engagement

Businesses can also use Social Media as a way of engaging with a large number of customers. Before Social Media, businesses would use print or telephone to engage with their customers. These options are still available and should still be used. However the use of Social Media allows businesses to very quickly gauge reaction to a new product or service, a new advert or the latest promotion. Many large businesses seek and receive an immediate reaction on the latest TV advert that they run. If you use Social Media channels to involve your customers and make changes based on their response, you are likely to have more loyal customers.

3 Find New Customers

Use Social Media to find new customers. Tools are available to search for what people are talking about on Social Media. I search for anybody that mentions Twitter Training within 50 miles of Oxford. I can see comments from people who are advertising Twitter Training courses (my competitors) as well as people who are seeking Twitter Training (my potential customers). By engaging my potential customers in conversation, I can build trust and interest in the services I offer.

There are many other reasons to engage with Social Media – many will be covered in more detail when we discuss your aims in Chapter 3. Most businesses should consider how Social Media can be used as part of their marketing mix in some form. One of the issues that businesses have with Social Media is that they lose control of their brand. The thing to remember is that people can talk about your brand using Social Media whether you engage or not. Which is better? You talking with your audience or your audience talking about you without you knowing what they are saying?

Think of Social Media as a great big face to face networking room or meeting room. If you stand on the edge of the room and tell everybody about your latest product or service, you are likely to be ignored. If you get into the room, ask questions and find out what other people think, you are more likely to be able to talk about your product or service. You are 'engaging'.

1.3 What is a Strategy?

A Strategy is a blueprint for growing your business. A Social Media Strategy can be seen as a plan for using Social Media as a marketing tool within your business. The Strategy will identify which channels you are going to use, what you are going to say, how you are going to say it, who is going to say it, why it will be said and what the result should be.

I believe that a number of factors should be taken into account when creating your Social Media Strategy as shown in Figure 1. Every business will have a unique Strategy based on:

- How the business is currently marketed
- The aims of the business
- The audience
- The Social Media channels currently available
- What the business can talk about
- The resources available in the business
- How success is measured.

Each of these factors needs to be considered and each will contribute to the overall Social Media Strategy you develop. We will consider each of these in turn as we work through the book and you will be asked to fill in worksheets for your own business. The elements cannot be considered in isolation. As we progress through the workbook, you may find you need to return to some of the worksheets

to amend them based on your increased understanding

I believe that a Social Media Strategy should be created with all parts of the business in mind. As you work through this book, I would recommend and encourage you to share your findings, observations and ideas with other members of the business at all levels.

Figure 1 - Social Media Strategy

1.4 Social Media Channels

As I have already stated, I believe there are a number of channels that can fall into the term 'Social Media'. The channels can be grouped as shown in Figure 2:

- **Social Networking** - including Twitter, LinkedIn, Facebook and Google+
- **Blogs** - regular commentary or opinions relating to your business, normally 200 – 500 words long
- **Videos** – A video is a very accessible medium for helping people to understand your business
- **Images** – a way of sharing images of your products or business personality
- **Social Bookmarks** – a method for other people to promote your website or blog
- **Other Channels** – such as Forums and location marketing tools
- **Website** – Your website is central to all Social Media. If somebody starts to talk to you using social networking or internet forums, watches your video, listens to a podcast or reads an article, the next step would be to go and look at your website. Your website needs to give the visitor a call to action, whether this is to buy a product or service or contact you.

We will consider all of these channels in much more detail in Chapter 6.

1.5 Some Numbers

It is interesting to look at the numbers of people using Social Media to understand the importance of this new medium. Do note, however, numbers by their very nature will be soon out of date.

- **Facebook** (August 2015)
  There are over 1.49 billion monthly active users
- **Twitter** (August 2015)
  There are over 316 million monthly active users
- **LinkedIn** (August 2015)
  Over 380 million people are registered on LinkedIn with around 97 million using it actively each month. It is now a standard part of the recruitment process
- **Google+ (April 2015)**
  Officially Google+ has over 2.5 billion users, but a report in early 2015 suggests that only 4 – 6 million people engage, interact and post publicly on Google+
- **Blogs** (September 2014)
  31% of the Fortune 500 companies are actively blogging
- **YouTube** (October 2015)
  YouTube has over a billion users – almost a third of all people on the Internet – and every day, people watch hundreds of millions of hours of YouTube videos and generate billions of views

These numbers are growing all the time. The speed at which people are using Social Media is just amazing. Your past, current and prospective customers are going to be using Social Media. They may already be using it to talk about you or your competitors. You need to be aware of what they are saying and be prepared to talk to and engage with them. Let's start with having a look at how you are currently telling people about your business.

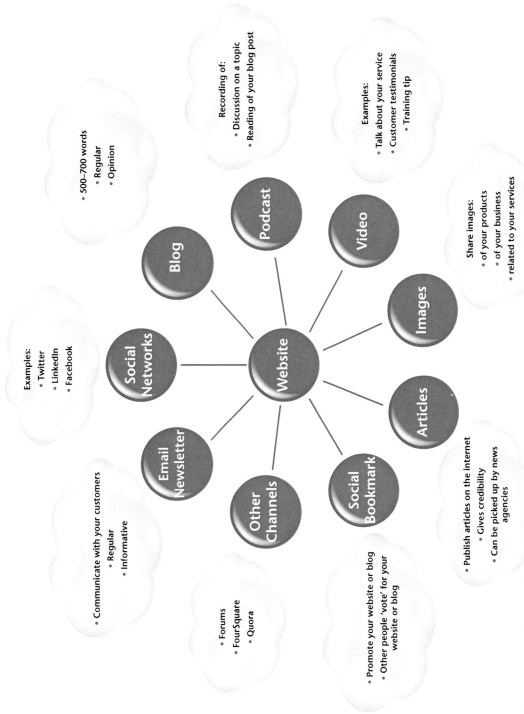

Figure 2 – Social Media Channels

CHAPTER TWO

According to the Chartered Institute of Marketing, marketing is:

"The management process responsible for identifying, anticipating and satisfying customer requirements profitably."

You need to have the answer that your customer wants at the time that your customer wants it. Ten or fifteen years ago, you would be marketing directly to your customer by focusing on the benefits that you can give your customer. You may have done this through television ads, newspaper ads, leaflets and exhibitions. These would have been targeted at a specific group of people. You may have got some referrals from people to their direct contacts.

As the Internet grew popular, your website may have become the focus of your marketing. This would be seen by anybody who searched for you or your product on the Internet – but this relied on you reaching that elusive goal of appearing on the first page of search results.

These are all still good and accurate ways of marketing your business – along with email and newsletters and the way you talk to your customers and answer the phone. We now also have the opportunity to talk to a great number of potential customers through Social Media. What is even more powerful is that Social Media allows people we may not even know to talk about us to others.

Before you start down the road of Social Media though, you need to take stock of what you are doing now. You need to review all of your current marketing including a review of what you are doing, how your business is perceived by others, the values of your business and how your values are integrated into your marketing material. It is important to understand how much time your marketing takes, how much it costs and how successful it is. This chapter considers your current marketing channels in more detail.

2.1 Brand

The brand of a business is more than just your logo. It is everything that tells your audience who you are and what you stand for. This includes all your marketing (including your Social Media) and every interaction with your audience. My brand includes my logo, my company name, my personal picture, my appearance, my voice and tone and the language that I use. It is important to me that I appear supportive, approachable and friendly. I need to talk the language that my audience will understand. There is no point talking 'geek' to somebody who is technophobic.

You and your staff are a key part of your brand and how they appear to your audience reflects on your brand. The appearance of your staff and the quality of your written word are both important parts of your brand. In terms of Social Media, the photos that your employees use on an individual business profile reflect on your brand and how they write their status updates reflects on your brand.

For Example

- During one of my face to face workshops, I searched LinkedIn for certain keywords. The results returned included a Business Development Manager for a large corporate company. The reaction of the people in the room to the photo associated with the Business Development Manager was interesting. The photo was clearly a holiday snap and did not present a professional image. The consensus in the workshop was that they would not do business with this individual, a split second decision made purely on the photo.

In a similar way, you need to consider how the quality of your written word in your Social Media updates reflects your brand. We can forgive the odd typing error such as typing "thsi" instead of "this", but using the wrong version of "your" or "their" consistently could reflect badly on your brand. Would you swear when in a client meeting? Then why do people do this on Social Media? How does this reflect their brand?

Values

Make sure you and your employees who are going to be doing the marketing or using the Social Media channels have a good understanding of the values of your business. Do you all know what your business stands for? Your values should be communicated through each contact you have with your customers and others and the way that you do business. All communication, both external and internal should be based around your identified values.

Example 1

IBM publishes its values as:
- **Dedication to every client's success**
- **Innovation that matters, for our company and for the world**
- **Trust and personal responsibility in all relationships**

Example 2

Concise Training's values are:
- **Flexible**
- **Quality**
- **Knowledgeable**
- **Helpful**
- **Positive ('can do' attitude)**
- **Value for Money**

I want to ensure that these values are present through all my marketing. I do my best to be responsive and helpful by email. I'm happy to share information using blogs, my website, Social Media and email. In a training workshop, I will share information around the topic (explain the importance of keywords, for example, in a LinkedIn workshop). It is important to me to always be positive on Social Media. I may occasionally be critical, but I do this in a constructive way. I use Social Media primarily for business and while I am flexible, I don't want to appear to be available 'out of hours', so I rarely use Twitter, for example, outside working hours. I use Twitter to share information and to be helpful, so will try to answer people's queries and will share information from others.

Exercise 1: Your Values

Write down four to six words or phrases that you think are the most important when you are conducting business. Typical words and phrases may include 'honesty', 'innovation', 'flexibility', 'quality', 'treating everybody with dignity and respect'.

1	
2	
3	
4	
5	
6	

2.2 Success

According to the Oxford English Dictionary success is:

- **The accomplishment of an aim or purpose**
- **The good or bad outcome of an undertaking.**

I think these are interesting definitions. Do you set yourself a target for each marketing activity that you undertake? Is there a reason behind starting the activity or are you doing it because someone told you that you should or it 'seemed like a good idea at the time'?

Depending on who you are and your business, the aim of a marketing activity doesn't always have to be monetary. As a sole trader, sometimes it is a success to get out from behind my screen and talk to real people at a face to face networking meeting. If I feel motivated or ready to get back to my screen afterwards then to me it has been a 'success'. I just need to decide whether that 'success' is worth the money that has been spent to achieve it.

I really believe that each business and probably each employee of a business will have their own aims and own measures of success. It is important that in general the aims of the marketing activity are going in the same direction as the overall aims of the business.

Make sure you regularly review each marketing activity to understand whether the original aims (assuming there were some) are still valid and whether you are still achieving those aims and working towards your business goals.

Your business goals should be specific and incorporate an action for achievement. "To achieve 20% next year" isn't enough. You may want to say "To achieve 20% growth by selling 10% more to existing customers and getting 10% more customers". Your marketing activities should then be directly related to selling 10% more to existing customers and gaining 10% new customers.

Exercise 2: Business Goals

Write down your Business Goals

2.3 Marketing Activities

You now need to review how you currently market your business. You need to understand how much each type of marketing costs, how much time you or your employees spend on the activity and how successful your marketing activities are. You may currently use a number of activities to market your business including:

- Face To Face Networking
- Business Card
- Website
- Print Advertising
- Leaflets
- Internet Advertising
- Exhibitions
- Email
- Telesales.

What is the cost of each of these marketing outlets in terms of time and money? When working out the monetary cost, include all the costs. For example, if you use face to face networking as a marketing activity, make sure you include the cost of breakfast or lunch as well as the cost of petrol. Similarly, when you work out the amount of time you or your employees spend on networking, include all of the time, including the time taken getting to and from the meeting, the time spent at the meeting and any follow up you need to do.

As part of this review, I want you to examine the return on investment (ROI) of each marketing activity that you undertake. How much business and how many contacts do you get from each marketing activity? How many referrals do you get? How often is your brand mentioned?

Work through Exercise 3 to see how successful your current marketing is.

Exercise 3:
Overview of Current Marketing

In this exercise you'll look at an overview of your current marketing activities in terms of cost, time and success. There are four parts to this exercise:

1. Look at the sheet on page 21. Along the bottom of each column, fill in any marketing activities that you do. I have filled in the first for you.

2. Now, consider the amount of money you spend on each activity. Shade each blue 'Cost' column to represent the proportion of money that you spend on each activity. For example, if you only have two marketing activities, a website and an advert in your local magazine, you would have two columns. If you spend £2000 on your website each year and £500 on advertising in the local magazine, you need to shade 80% of the website column and 20% of the advertising column. To complete this exercise, you may have to take some time to calculate your costs of marketing first!

3. Next, consider how much time you spend on each activity. Shade each green 'Time' column to indicate the proportion of the total time you and your employees spend on each activity.

4. Now, consider how successful each activity is. To do this, you need to calculate how many sales, referrals and brand mentions you get as a result of each activity. Shade each black 'Success' column to represent the proportion of success of each activity.

On page 22, I've created one as an example for you. As you can see my marketing was primarily split between my website, face to face networking and my newsletter. I also do Social Media marketing which is not included here. By performing this exercise I realised that I needed to spend less time and money on face to face networking and put more resource into making my already successful website even better. I haven't stopped face to face networking but I have been more selective with the networks I attend and the amount I spend on them.

Hopefully this exercise has confirmed what you already knew – or has raised some issues for you to look at. Were all your marketing activities returning the appropriate return on investment? If not, you may want to consider whether you should keep spending money on the same thing to get the same result. When I undertook this exercise, I realised that one networking group that I belonged to had been very successful for the first couple of years, but more recently hadn't given me any new clients or new contacts; it was time to try something new.

As part of this exercise, you need to determine what time and money you can divert to Social Media. You may want to include Social Media in addition to what you are currently doing, but it is more likely it will need to replace something that is not working for you. People often say to me that Social Media takes up too much time. My response is how much time and money do you spend on other marketing activities like traditional advertising, exhibiting or networking events? Could some of that time be spent on Social Media?

I am not suggesting that you stop all your current marketing and concentrate on Social Media. I firmly believe that Social Media should become an integrated part of your marketing mix. Over time the percentage of your marketing mix that is Social Media may increase.

Make a note of any action points that you need to take as a result of this exercise.

Marketing Cost (C), Time (T) and Success (S)

Marketing Cost (C), Time (T) and Success (S) – Concise Training Example

2.4 Social Media Marketing

Clearly this workbook is all about Social Media Marketing and don't worry we will get to focus on developing your use of Social Media soon! Before we do, it is worth taking a few minutes to think about any Social Media that is currently happening in your business. You may find if you ask around that there are people using LinkedIn already; there may be people already using Twitter.

It is important at this stage to understand what Social Media is being used in your business and be able to judge its current use against your values and brand. As we work through the remainder of this book, don't forget to go back and change or develop what you discover here.

Have a look at Exercise 4.

Put yourself in the shoes of your audience and consider how the Social Media that you are already doing reflects upon the brand and values of your business. Also, start thinking about how you measure the success of your Social Media – if in fact you measure success at all. If you don't use Social Media yet, or don't understand what all these channels are, don't worry because they are all discussed in detail in Chapter 6.

Exercise 4: Review of Current Social Media Marketing

Use the form below to rate any Social media channels that are currently being used in the business. Do they reflect your brand and your values? Rate the success of your Social Media efforts on a scale of 1 – 10 where 1 is unsuccessful and 10 is very successful. Which activities contribute to your business goals and which do not?

Form of Marketing	Use (√)	Reflects Brand	Reflects Values	Success 1-10	How is it contributing to your business goals?	Action required?
Blog(s)						
Email Newsletter						
Video						
Podcast						
LinkedIn						
Facebook						
Twitter						
Google +						
Internet Forum(s) Which ones?						
Social Bookmarking Which ones?						
Other						

2.5 Summary of Chapter 2

In this chapter you looked at the first circle in the Strategy chart – Review. You have clarified the goals, brand and values of your business and reviewed all the marketing activities you are using, in light of these business goals, brand and values. You have determined how successful your marketing activities are and you have also looked at how you currently use Social Media marketing. This will change and develop as you work through the remainder of this book.

In Chapter 3 you'll be looking at your reasons for using Social Media and what you want to achieve.

CHAPTER THREE

What do you want to get out of the Social Media marketing effort? Why do you want to use it? Ultimately you probably want to get more business and increase your presence on the Internet, but what short term and long term goals do you want to achieve through your use of Social Media? You need to have some real reasons or objectives for your Social Media use other than 'because everybody else seems to be using it"!

Your objectives for using Social Media should be linked to your business goals, but will depend on the size and type of your business.

Size of business

The size of your business and your resources will have an impact on which Social Media tools you can use. Although you may wish to grow your business, you have to be realistic about the amount of new customers you can cope with and the amount of Social Media Marketing that you can do.

Type of business

In my opinion, the use of Social Media is applicable to most types of businesses, but your business should have an Internet presence to make the most of it. My local window cleaner might receive referrals via Twitter, but will he actually look at Twitter to see those referrals? On the other hand, I do know of a small carpet cleaning firm who have found the use of Social Media very successful for building brand awareness and generating referrals. The firm also uses Twitter to arrange additional appointments. If the owner has arranged an appointment in Cheltenham on a Tuesday afternoon, he uses Twitter to arrange a job to fill the morning.

Your objectives for using Social Media will change and develop over time as your business grows. I suggest you think about short term and long term objectives.

For Example

- Initially I wanted to use Social Media to build my brand, by sharing information which would give me credibility as someone knowledgeable about IT applications. Over time, people have asked me IT related questions using Social Media tools and I have received referrals directly through Social Media.

- Some businesses might want to use Social Media to drive traffic to their website. I am working with a firm that sells pewter miniatures. We need to make sure that people are aware that the website exists and what it sells. We can drive traffic to the website through coordinated use of Social Media.

A different reason may be to provide customer service. For other businesses, it could be something unique to them, such as a sandwich shop taking orders through Social Media.

Depending upon your objectives, you will need to select different Social Media tools and use them in different ways. Note that here we are talking about your reasons for using Social Media as a method of engaging and communicating with your audience. Remember, your Social Media aims will be linked to your business goals – which you identified in Chapter 2 - and should be considered as one of the ways of achieving them.

Your objectives for using Social Media could be:

- **Brand or reputation building or developing the personality of a business**
- **Driving traffic to your website**
- **Increasing footfall in a retail shop**
- **Sharing interests, news, tips or information (yours or others)**
- **Increasing visibility or extending influence**
- **Getting feedback from customers or providing customer service**
- **Finding out information about your potential customers.**
- **Advertising events and training courses**
- **Promoting offers**
- **Developing awareness about products or services**
- **Having conversations with people and developing engagement**
- **Gaining support from others**
- **Learning new techniques.**

Many of your reasons will overlap and one may result in the next. The ways you use Social Media should be complimentary to help you achieve your overall business goals.

Now complete Exercise 5 to identify why you are thinking of using Social Media for your business.

Exercise 5: Why Use Social Media?

1 **Have another look at Exercise 2, in which you identified your business goals. Review this exercise (or complete it if you skipped past it!)**

2 **Think about what you want to get out of your Social Media use in relation to achieving your business goals. Complete the following steps:**

a Look at the suggestions of reasons for using Social Media listed in the following table and add any of your reasons that are not covered

b Indicate which of the reasons listed you want to focus on in the short term (next six months) and which you want to think about in the long term (two years)

c Now give your short term focuses a priority – which is the most important? Give this some thought – you should not have them all listed as a priority of '1'.

Keep coming back to these objectives to review the list as you progress through this book.

Now you have some initial thoughts about what you are trying to get out of Social Media, you need to start thinking about who you want to engage with when using Social Media.

What am I going to Use Social Media for?	Short Term (√)	Long Term (√)	Priority
Brand or reputation building			
Driving traffic to your website			
Increasing footfall in a retail shop			
Sharing your news			
Sharing other's news			
Sharing tips			
Increasing visibility			
Extending influence			
Getting feedback from customers			
Sharing interests			
Bringing personality to a business			
Sharing information			
Providing customer service			
Advertising events and training courses			
Promoting offers			
Developing awareness about products or services			
Having conversations with people			
Developing engagement			
Gaining support from others			
Developing new business			
Learning new techniques			
Finding out information about your potential customers			

CHAPTER FOUR

Just as with offline marketing, when you're starting out with Social Media, you need to identify your target audience. Your potential audience on Social Media is likely to be larger than your offline marketing audience. Social Media makes it easier for more people, including your competitors and other members of the public, to find and connect with you. It is also makes it easier for you to reach out to more people. Your audience could include:

- **Customers (Current, Potential and Past)**
- **Suppliers**
- **Influencers**
- **Brand Ambassadors**
- **Staff**
- **Business Partners**
- **Personal Contacts**
- **Competitors.**

To explain these groups further:

4.1 Customers

You want to talk to those people who are going to or have already bought from you. It is always easier to sell to those who have bought once already. Social Media can be a great way of staying in contact with customers who have bought from you before.

You can use Social Media to identify people who are talking about their need for your product or service. Use tools like Google Alerts, SocialMention, HootSuite, Tweetdeck and others to listen to what people are saying about your products or services and react and respond appropriately. For more information on these, check them out on line.

You can also learn a lot from talking to your customers on Social Media. You should record information learnt from these conversations on a database or Customer Relationship Management (CRM) system. This information will allow you to offer your customers a more personalised service in the future.

You need to think about where your customers are, as this will affect the Social Media Channels you should use. A business based entirely in a set location, such as a shop, may want to focus their Social Media geographically. A business based more nationally or globally using an e-commerce shop will be more concerned with national or global Social Media. Some businesses will need to use a combination of approaches.

You should also consider whether you are in a Business to Business (B2B), Business to Consumer (B2C) or Charitable environment. A different approach to Social Media will be required, depending on who your customers are.

For Example

- ECCO Oxford started using Social Media for marketing at the beginning of 2011. They started slowly and gradually grew the number of channels and amount of time and therefore the size of their audience. By the end of 2011, ECCO Oxford was comfortable that Social Media Marketing was providing a return on investment in terms of sales and customer service. During 2012, more people in the company were encouraged to take part in the Social Media communication. It also became clear that there was a new business opportunity based on the engagement that they were having with their audience.

Social Media is a great opportunity to talk to your prospective customers. Why not use Social Media to ask your customers what different products or services they would like you to provide, or what your customer service team can do to help them? Ask your customers what they think of your new shop or website design, etc.

4.2 Suppliers

Social Media is an amazing source of information. You can find people to support your business based on the recommendations of others, find information about the latest developments in your industry and see how your suppliers are doing. Share your supplier's success stories with your own audience. Engaging with your suppliers on Social Media will deepen relationships with them.

4.3 Influencers

Your influencers are the people who may not buy your services or product directly, but are in a good position to recommend you to others. However, be aware that influencers could also be negative. An influencer will generally have a large number of followers and will be able to spread your message to a wide audience.

For example, a charity wanted to find a celebrity patron. Having developed a presence on Twitter, they drew up a list of possible celebrities and started to listen to and talk to, potential 'targets'. They were able to develop this engagement far more easily than if they tried through traditionally channels.

I worked with another charity, the European Doctors Orchestra. This is a group of doctors from all over Europe who come together twice a year to put on a concert with proceeds going to charity. I started working with them at the beginning of October for a concert in Newcastle at the end of November. By using Twitter and Facebook, they were able to engage with other orchestras and music leaders including London Symphony, Northern Sinfonia and the music press. These groups were able to promote their concert to their much wider audience.

4.4 Brand Ambassadors

Your Brand Ambassadors are people who may or may not buy your services. They often come from your customer base but could also be somebody who knows you or your business well but may never have bought your product or service.

Your brand ambassador is somebody who is always positive about your brand and will jump in to defend you against criticism as well as promote you to others. You may want to think about giving your brand ambassadors special attention in the form of prior knowledge of products or services, trial access to new products or services or rewards programmes.

4.5 Staff

Some larger businesses find Social Media to be a very good way of communicating internally with staff. Is Social Media an appropriate medium for you to use to communicate with your staff? You may want your staff to use Social Media to communicate with their individual business contacts. You can then use an overall business account to promote interesting or relevant conversations. If you have sales staff, they may want to use Social Media to announce that they are in a particular geographical location. This may give them the opportunity to arrange additional appointments.

Social Media is a very successful and cost effective way of recruiting staff, so encourage your HR department to use it as well.

4.6 Business Partners

Social Media is a great way to support your Business Partners and share their knowledge and expertise with your contacts. By working together you can reach a much larger audience.

For example, I was an associate with Right Angle Consultants In February 2012, the partners and associates of Right Angle Consultants together wrote a book to support Business Growth. By all the associates working together to promote the book and generate a buzz on Social Media, we were able to reach many more people than if we had each tried to talk to our individual networking groups. We were also able to develop a supportive community amongst the associates by developing a 'caring-sharing' mindset.

4.7 Personal Contacts

Social Media is a good way of keeping in contact with people you have met in other ways. I keep in touch with people that I met face to face several years ago through Social Media. It allows me to see what they are doing and I can offer support as appropriate. Likewise they do the same for me. I have recently received referrals from somebody I first met several years ago and kept in contact with using Social Media. Without the power of Social Media, it is likely that this relationship would have died over time.

4.8 Competitors

Remember that nearly everything can be seen by your competitors. I highly recommend that you listen to what your competitors are saying on Social Media; and remember that they will be listening to you! You can learn from your competitors but do be aware of client confidentiality. I know more than one person who has a public list on Twitter named 'clients'; because this is public, anybody can see which clients are in this list!

Exercise 6: Audience Groups

To find out your audience groups:

1 Look at who you are currently talking to via email, newsletter or networking and capture which groups make up your current audience.

2 Listen to find out who is talking about you on Social Media. You can use tools like www.socialmention.com to find out when you and your business are mentioned in blogs and on Social Networking sites.

3 Consider who might make up your audience as your business goes forward.

4 Think about who you would like to talk about your business. Really think outside the box here – you may be able to get your business in front of some really useful people using Social Media.

5 Look at the circles. Fill in the circles with some information about your audience. You may want to describe the characteristics of each group or you may find it easier to give some examples of your audience in each group.

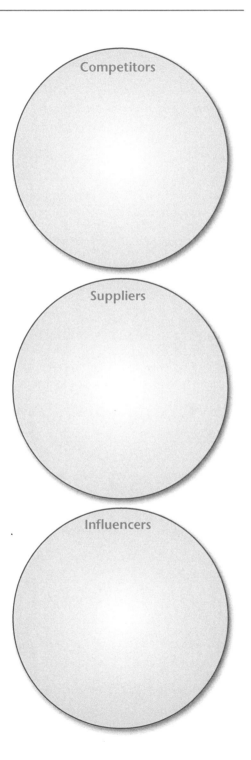

Competitors

Suppliers

Influencers

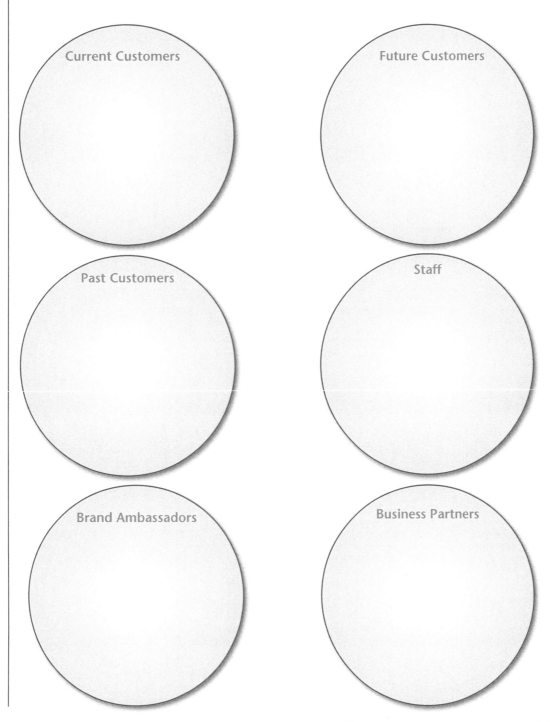

Current Customers

Future Customers

Past Customers

Staff

Brand Ambassadors

Business Partners

4.9 Where Does Your Audience Hang Out?

Now you know your different audience groups, you need to think about where they hang out, because different people use different forms of Social Media. There is no point in having a massive presence on one form of Social Media if none of your audience is present.

If you sell primarily to consumers, you may find that they mainly use Facebook. If your audience is mostly other businesses, you may find LinkedIn more appropriate. Do your audience use mobile technology? You may find you can talk to your Influencers using Twitter, which is a great way of getting past the 'gate keeper'. Are your competitors already using Social Media effectively or will you be breaking new ground in this arena?

It may be that your audience is spread out amongst the Social Media sites, they may be clustered on one or two, or perhaps they don't use Social Media yet. You also need to think about trends and how things are changing. The use of YouTube is growing at a fantastic rate, so this might be the most appropriate medium for you. Remember also the need to be found on Search Engines - using Social Media will help people find you online.

For Example

● Many accountancy firms use LinkedIn and Twitter as their primary Social Media. In 2011, I worked with Accountants A. As part of developing their Social Media strategy, we analysed their potential audience. We discovered that they had a number of private clients abroad. This indicated that they should develop a Facebook presence, as this was the channel of choice for those private clients who lived abroad.

Exercise 7: Where Does Your Audience Hang Out?

Now you have identified your audience groups, you need to research where they can currently be found in the Social Media space, so work through this exercise.

1. Take some examples of the best, worst and average businesses or individuals in each audience group. Look at the websites of each of the examples. Do they have links to Social Networking accounts (Twitter, LinkedIn, Facebook, Google+ and YouTube)? If they do, is the link on their Home page or on the Contact page of their website? Are they currently active on the Social Networking Profile? Do they have a blog?

2. If you don't find Social Media links on their websites, search for each of the audience examples on Twitter, LinkedIn, Facebook, Google+, YouTube and Blogging sites. Use www.socialmention.com to find out where and when your audience groups are **mentioned in the Social Media space.**

3. Capture this information in the table on the following page. How are you currently engaging with the audience group and how do you think you might engage using Social Media? At this stage, this may only be a 'gut feel' and you will need to revisit this as you develop your Social Media Strategy.

Now you have identified the audience that you are going to engage with using Social Media, you need to consider what combination of Social Media channels will be most suitable for your business.

In Chapter 6, we will consider each Social Media channel in detail. As you understand how each channel can be used, you will start to see how you can use the channel to achieve your aims and engage with your audience.

First, we need to understand the concept of keywords – which is what we'll do in the next chapter.

Audience Group	Example	Current Marketing or Engagement	Social Networking: Twitter LinkedIn Facebook Google+	Mobile Technology	Video	Comments
Current Customer						
Potential Customer						
Past Customer						
Supplier						
Influencer						
Brand Ambassador						
Staff						
Business Partner						
Personal Contact						
Competitor						

Keywords are those words your audience will use to find you using search engines and Social Media. You need to take some time to identify what keywords or keyword phrases are most appropriate for your business, for your website and your Social Media.

Find and use keyword phrases on your website:

1. You want certain audience groups to look at and act on your website. You need to understand what keyword phrases these audience groups will use to find you. They may not be phrases that you use to describe your business – they need to be words that your audience will use.

2. There are tools to help you understand the volumes of people that search for phrases and the competitive nature of phrases. You are aiming for a relatively high search volume with low competition – lots of people searching for a phrase that is only used on a few websites. Be realistic though - if you try to achieve a keyword phrase that is searched for 100,000 times a month, would you be able to cope with 1,000 new clients (at a conservative conversion rate)?

3. Each page of your website should have its own set of keywords. Using the keywords in key places of the web page will help the search engines to rank you higher. These key places include the Page Title, the Description, the URL, Headings and content of the page. It is also important to include relevant keywords in text (called Alt Text) that is attached to each image on the page. The Alt Text on an image allows both search engines and screen readers to read what the image is about. Note that keywords should not be put onto Alt Text unless they are relevant to the image and the page the image is on.

4. Certain keyword phrases are harder to optimise than others and some are just not searched for. It may well be easy to get on page one of your search engine results for a phrase that nobody searches for.

Find and use keyword phrases in your Social Media:

1. The keywords that you use in Social Media may be similar to those you use on your website, but are likely to be shorter phrases or individual keywords.

2. Use Social Media to listen for people's conversations about your proposed keywords. You may find that your keyword list needs to be refined or shortened to return useful information. Once you find people talking about keywords, you can join in the conversation. I recommend that you do not immediately try to sell, but rather share information and promote trust.

3. Combinations of individual keywords can be used to 'tag' content on Social Media. A 'tag' is a word that is attached to a piece of content which search engines use to identify what the content is about. You can use tags on blog posts, videos and audio files

4. Use your identified keywords in your Social Media content. This will include the titles of your blogs, your profiles and your status updates. We talk further about status updates in the next chapter.

Exercise 8: Keywords for Social Media

When you designed your website, you should have identified a set of keyword phrases. If not, I suggest you talk to your website designer about this. In this exercise we want to identify your keywords for use on Social Media.

Write down 7 phrases that you are going to start listening for and talking about on Social Media. You may find that you listen for and talk about the same things – or maybe not. We will explore content more in Chapter 8.

	Listening	Talking
1		
2		
3		
4		
5		
6		
7		

Figure 3: Social Media Channels

CHAPTER SIX

There are a number of different channels to access Social Media, as you can see in Figure 3. Each has its own advantages, disadvantages and resource requirements and they are all connected together and should all be linked to your Website. The use of each Social Media channel will improve your overall internet footprint, which can help to improve the chances of your site appearing on the first page of Google. You need to understand how different combinations of Social Media channels can help you achieve your short and long term objectives.

I am a firm believer in reusing information. If I write a blog post, I will promote that blog post on Social Media. I may well use the contents of the blog post in bite sized chunks on my Social Networking sites (LinkedIn, Twitter, Facebook, Google+). I could also create a podcast of the blog post or use a video to illustrate the point of the blog post. I would encourage my followers to use Social Bookmarking to push the blog post further up the search engine rankings. I can pin the image I used in the blog post onto a Pinterest board. I could use Internet forums to promote my blog post and publish a version of the blog post on an article publishing site like Ezine Articles (http://ezinearticles.com/).

However, it is important, in my opinion, to remember who your audience is on each Social Media channel. It is tempting to register with each of the channels and then use one of the many tools that are available, to push the same content out on each channel. I recommend that you use the available management tools to post updates tailored to each channel.

An update is a short text based entry using one of the Social Media channels that tells everybody you are connected with, or who follows you, something that you think they will find interesting. The word "interesting" is subjective - some people share what they had for lunch – some people give tips or information, some people offer their personal opinions on absolutely anything. It is entirely up to you what you share! The update can include images or links to websites (your own or others). To engage with others, you can reply to updates or offer your opinion on their updates. Different Social Media channels are used to offer a different tone or type of update.

To get the best out of the different Social Media opportunities, you need to take the time to understand the differences between the audiences on each site and the type of update that will appeal to them. Each site allows a different length of update, so make use of what is available. For example, Twitter updates must be 140 characters or less, but LinkedIn allows you to use over 400 characters in the update; Facebook and Google+ are almost unlimited.

I have included Email newsletters in Figure 3. They aren't strictly Social Media, but they are a very important way of regularly connecting with your contact base. You can often use the same content in your Email newsletter as you have posted using Social Media. My newsletter will frequently include a link to a couple of relevant blog posts as well as links to my website, my Social Networking (LinkedIn, Twitter, Facebook, Google+) sites and any videos or podcasts that I have recently produced.

We will now look at each of the channels in turn. For each one we will look at a brief description of the channel, why you should consider using it, the audience for the tool, the time you should spend, how you are going to measure success of its use and the potential cost of using the tool. For each of the main channels, I will give you examples of how businesses of all sizes are successfully using the tool.

As you work through the channels, fill in Exercise 9 on page 69. For each channel, you need to decide:

- **Whether you are going to use it in the short, medium or long term**
- **How much time you are going to allocate for the channel and when**
- **How much money you are going to allocate to using the channel**
- **Why you think you should use the channel and who your audience is**
- **What you are going to talk about (there is more about content in Chapter 8)**
- **How you are going to measure success of using the channel**
- **Any training, information or people resources you need.**

6.1 Website

You need to ensure that your website reflects your business brand and values and is written for your audience. I am a firm believer that your website needs to be central to all of your Social Media Marketing. If somebody gets to know you through Social Media, they will often look at your website before choosing to buy. Your website gives your business credibility and should have links to all of your Social Media channels.

You need to consider how often your website will be viewed on a mobile device. If your audience is likely to use mobile devices, you may need to adjust the design of your website to include a clearer 'call to action', larger easy to use buttons and less text. At the very least, your website code may need to be adjusted to ensure that it can be displayed on a variety of mobile devices.

Audience

The audience of your website will potentially be all of your audience groups that you identified in Chapter 4; you will also need to write your copy so that Search Engines can read your site. Your website should be accessible, so screen readers must be able to read it as well as people suffering from red/ green colour blindness and other disabilities.

Some guidelines:

- **Your keyword phrase for each page should be included in 10% of the content of the page copy**
- **Include your keyword phrase in the headings and sub headings on the page (if appropriate)**

- **All images should have alternative text (Alt Text) identified (with keywords if appropriate)**
- **Count how many times you use words like 'You' and 'We' on the page. You should aim to write words like 'You' four times as often as you use words like 'We'**
- **The copy should be written for your human audience and should be benefit driven**
- **Your contact information should be available in the top part of your website.**

Time and Cost

I suggest you regularly spend time refreshing the content of your website and ensuring that it accurately reflects the services you provide. This could be once a day, every six months or more, depending on whether you update your website yourself or have an external supplier do this for you. The cost will vary accordingly. Of course if you have a blog (see section 6.2) on your website, this will refresh it.

Measurement

Use Google Analytics, a free tool, to monitor hits to your website, bounce rate (people who come to a page and leave again) and referral sources – how people have found your website. Looking at this data can indicate areas of your website that you need to improve or leave alone depending on success.

6.2 Blogs

A blog is like a diary on the internet. Blog posts should be approximately 500 – 700 words long (on average – you may find occasions when they need to be longer and this is fine), can be on any subject and should include at least one image. From a business perspective, it is more beneficial for your blog posts to be related to your business or area of specialism, but you may want to write about an area of interest. Blogs are not so much updated as added to – a blog becomes a stream of 500 – 700 word separate articles.

Blogs should not be used to sell, as people will only continue to read your blog if it contains interesting thoughts or useful information. New blog articles can be created as often as you wish – while some people post blogs every day, once a week or once a fortnight is a good frequency to aim for if you are starting out. You may want to consider asking somebody to write a guest post on your blog to increase the number of your posts.

Blogs create engagement as people can comment on them. You can request comments at the end of your posts by asking 'What do you think?' or 'Have you had any experience of this?' Make sure that you respond to any comments and do check and remove spam comments you receive.

You should use your blog in conjunction with your other Social Media. Do this by using your Social Networking feeds on LinkedIn, Facebook and Twitter to drive traffic to your blog and vice versa. Your blog should show your expertise, which will ultimately drive traffic to your website and from there to sales conversion - hopefully!

There are two main ways to create a blog:

- **Using a free tool like WordPress.org, Blogger or Tumblr**
- **Self-hosting a blog on your website.**

Although using a free tool is a great way of getting started with blogging, I strongly suggest that you consider quickly moving your blog to your own website. There are a number of reasons for this including:

- **Updating the blog will refresh your website which is good for SEO (Search Engine Optimisation)**
- **It is unclear who owns the content of a blog hosted by Wordpress.org or Blogger. Although to date, there have been no legal cases, the terms and conditions of WordPress and Blogger indicate that WordPress and Blogger own the Intellectual Property Rights of any content posted on their free hosting options.**
- **You have no control over a blog hosted by Wordpress.org or Blogger. If Wordpress.org or Blogger want to take down your site, you can't stop them from doing it.**
- **One of the reasons for having a blog is to get people to visit the other pages of your website. If it is difficult to see the link between two separate sites you are in danger of splitting your audience. If you are found via your blog, your audience may not find it easy to go to your website to find your services or products.**

Why Blog?

A blog gives you credibility. If you write about a subject on a regular basis, it shows that you know about the subject. It is a good idea to include your keywords in the title of your blog posts to improve the chances of them being found when people search. Titles that work well are 'How to ...' or '10 tips for ...' As these titles show, you can give away information in a blog. By sharing tips and giving away information you are providing value. This will make it more likely that people will read and share your blog. It also allows people to see you as an expert in your field.

Once a blog is written, it is on the Internet forever. I still have blog entries that I wrote two years ago appear in Search Engine results. When you write a blog you need to encourage people to look at it and respond. Think about:

- **The headline – make it catchy so it gets noticed**
- **The description – this needs to be provocative to draw attention to the rest of the post**
- **Posting when your audience are going to look at the site and not in the middle of the night**
- **Posting interesting articles regularly, as one off articles are unlikely to have the desired impact**
- **The content – for its accuracy**
- **Building relationships with others to get your post shared**

Make sure that people can subscribe to your blog using either RSS feeds or email subscription. Register your blog on blog directories to increase the likelihood of it being found.

Audience

As with your website, your blog will appeal to nearly all your audience groups. You want your past, present and future customers to read and share it. If you promote it on your Social Media channels, the general public, including your competitors, will be able to see it. You also want it to be read by Search Engines.

Time

Be careful not to get carried away. Keep your blog entries quite short, so that you are more likely to write them. You should set aside half to one hour a week for each post you want to write. You will find it easier to write your blog if you create a content strategy so that you can work out what you are going to write about a few months in advance – more on this in Chapter 8. You will also need to set aside time to monitor for and reply to, comments on your blog. If someone takes the time to write a comment, you should take the time to respond.

Cost

You may want to employ a copywriter to help you write your blog and you may have to pay for your website to be maintained. For you to write your own content, the only cost is your time.

Measurement

You can measure the success of your blog by looking at:

- **The number of hits to the page using Google Analytics**
- **The number of subscribers**
- **The number of comments you receive**

Examples

- Financial companies use blogs to comment on the latest news items. This provides them with a chance to show their expertise and can create a loyal following of clients and prospects. This ultimately builds their brand and drives traffic to their website.

- Technological businesses use blogs for a similar purpose. You are more likely to ask a company for help if you have been using their blogs as a resource.

- The CEO of a large hotel chain writes a weekly post describing his travels around the hotel network, offering some personal insights into events that happen on the way. This gives a personal side to the company which customers enjoy.

6.3 Email Newsletters

An email newsletter is a regular correspondence with your customers or potential customers - the image heavy emails that you receive in your inbox. You should only send a newsletter to people who have opted-in to receiving it. If you send your Email newsletter to people who have not requested it, you are in danger of being seen as sending spam which can damage your reputation and prevent you from using some Email newsletter systems. Your newsletter should provide value to your subscribers rather than selling to them. It should be interesting and be something that they want to read.

Make sure that your newsletter is professional – check for spelling and grammatical errors and make sure the links work. Your newsletter should be branded with your colours and logo and be clearly recognised as coming from your business. I recommend that you use an email system (for example Mail Chimp, Constant Contact or Just Add Content) to ensure that your newsletter can be opened in various email systems and the database is easy to manage.

Why send a Newsletter?

Although Email newsletters aren't strictly Social Media, I believe they are a very important part of marketing and form an integral part of engagement with your audience. A regular newsletter allows you to keep in regular touch with your audience.

For Example

- In the training industry, customers do buy again, but over a spread out period of time. If my customers regularly receive my newsletter, they are still getting value from me and will see what is going on with my business. When they do require more training I will be in 'front of mind' and easily accessible.

- A newsletter is a great way of telling people about different or new products and services you can provide. This book is about Social Media and I also offer Microsoft Office training. My newsletter caters to both markets. I can also use it to inform people about joint ventures or talks and workshops that I am promoting.

- A newsletter is also a good way of advertising your blog and other Social Media links that you have available.

Audience

If you are using the opt-in approach, your audience will generally be your past, present and future customers as well as contacts who have chosen to receive the newsletter. You may also advertise the signup form or back issues on Social Media.

Time

This is something else that can be outsourced. I usually spend half to one day a month on my newsletter. I recommend that you include your newsletter in your content strategy so that you have a good idea of what you are going to write about each month.

Cost

The cost is dependent on whether you outsource and how many subscribers you have. Some systems are free for a certain number of subscribers, so if you do it yourself, the only cost is your time.

Measurement

You can measure the success of your newsletter by:

- **Growth of your list**
- **Percentage opens**
- **Percentage of links clicked**
- **Feedback. I often meet people at networking meetings who tell me they like and read my newsletter. To me, this indicates success and that it is worth continuing as it forms part of my 'helpful' brand value.**

Examples

- Please sign up for my newsletter at www.concisetraining.net.
  Other newsletters that I like include Hexagon Web Works, Kuhnke Communication and Expertise on Tap.

6.4 Niche Channels

In this section, I have included channels that are a useful way to engage, but may not be applicable to every business. This section covers FourSquare, digital vouchers and QR codes.

6.4.1 Foursquare

Foursquare is most appropriate for restaurants, coffee shops and retail outlets. Businesses register their shop or restaurant with Foursquare and advertise within the shop that they are registered.

As a consumer, you 'check-in' to shops or restaurants – you update your friends on where you are. The more times you check-in to places, the more points or badges you earn. If you are the person who checks-in to a location most frequently, you become the 'Mayor'. This makes Foursquare into a game and appeals to the competitive nature of individuals who want to collect the most badges or become the Mayor at the most locations. Individuals are also encouraged to leave tips about the locations that they visit.

Shops and restaurants can also encourage people to check-in by offering discounts when certain conditions are met. For example, receive a 10% discount when you have checked-in 10 times or 'a free cup of coffee' if you are the Mayor of the restaurant.

Foursquare is particularly appropriate in the US and in larger towns and cities in the UK.

Why use Foursquare?

When somebody checks-in to your location, their friends are updated on Social Media sites. In these days of peer recommendation, if one person considers your business worth visiting, it is likely that others will too. In addition, every time your location is mentioned on Social Media sites, it increases Brand Recognition.

If you are giving away the chance of a free coffee to people who check-in, then people are more likely to go to your store than your competitor's store.

Audience

Foursquare works well for certain types of businesses, in certain locations, appealing to a certain demographic. There tends to be less concern about giving away personal information amongst a younger audience. An older demographic prefer not to tell people where they are. You will need to judge this based on your audience.

Time

Foursquare is quick and easy to set up and just requires you to monitor and respond to tips or comments. You may need to check when somebody has 'checked-in' or achieved the 'Mayor' status.

Cost

The cost is the cost of the promotion and the time spent on monitoring. FourSquare is currently free to join.

Measurement

- **Number of check-ins**
- **Number of tips and comments.**

Examples

- Starbucks offer a special badge after five check-ins
- Domino Pizza offered free pizza to the local Mayor on Wednesdays throughout the UK
- Gap offered a 25% discount for anybody who checked in to their store on a particular day.

6.4.2 Digital Vouchers

You may have received information about Groupon, Amazon Local or other digital vouchers through your email or seen them advertised on television.

For consumers, digital vouchers are a great method of receiving discounts on products or services. For a business, it is an opportunity to get your business known and get people through the door. As a business you agree with the digital voucher sales team what product or service you are going to offer, in what location, for how long and at what price. Make sure you remember to negotiate a maximum number of the product or service you can provide for sale. There have been instances where people have redeemed Groupon vouchers for more products than have been available.

Be aware that some digital voucher schemes will require you to create an offer resulting in a low or negative profit margin for each product or service. You are likely to be offering the product or service at a loss. You do need to be prepared to deal with high volumes as well - consumers like bargains!

Why use Digital Vouchers

Digital vouchers can be great for brand building and getting customers in through the door. You need to make sure that you have the systems in place to follow up with these customers so that they come back for more.

You need to understand who you are targeting the offer at. Existing customers may be included in the digital voucher email marketing – and you will need to allow them to take up the offer as well.

Audience

You want to target the offer at new customers. This can be a great way of breaking into a new location and letting people know about you. Existing customers and competitors may also be able to see the offer though.

Time

You will have to spend time with the sales team of the digital voucher scheme to ensure that the offer is right for your business. Do take this time to check as there have been incidents where the Groupon Sales Team has not informed the customer of all the potential pitfalls. Make sure that you have a team in place to service the vouchers. You will need people answering emails or telephones as well as providing the product or service.

Cost

You will have a cost of the discount. If you are selling a product, you will make little or no profit on it; if you are selling a service, the cost will just be your time.

Measurement

The main measure of success of a digital voucher campaign is not the number of vouchers you process but the number of repeat or new customers you get as a result. If you have many more people talking about your business, telling their friends and coming through your doors as a result of the campaign then it has been a success.

Examples

- A cup cake company set up a Groupon campaign to offer cup cakes at a discounted rate. They were inundated with requests and had to employ more staff to fulfil the requests as they had not agreed a maximum amount of vouchers with Groupon. Since they were making little profit on each order they lost thousands of pounds. This was a highly publicised case and fortunately they are still in business.

- A Beautician just starting in business advertised pedicures and manicures on Groupon. She got her brand name known in the local community and achieved a regular client base. This only cost her time in doing the treatments - time which she would otherwise have spent sitting waiting for clients.

- What's Ticking Today is a new daily digital voucher scheme aimed at offering the ability for merchants to provide local deals at a fair price of commission.

6.4.3 QR Codes

A 2D barcode is an image that contains information. One of the most common 2D barcodes is the QR (Quick Response) code which has square blocks at 3 corners of a square.

The information contained in a 2D bar code can be:

- **A URL to send a viewer directly to a website landing page or Facebook page**
- **A Vcard which sends information directly to the Contacts folder.**
- **A short message (SMS)**
- **Numbers such as a telephone number**
- **A link to a video**

You can create a QR code for free e.g. at http://www.qrstuff.com/ and all you need to scan and view is software or a smartphone app. The majority of these apps are free.

These QR code images can be displayed on print material, bill boards, clothes, skin (tattoos) and even projected onto buildings.

Why Use QR Codes

Every business should use QR codes on printed material. A business can use QR codes to encourage customers to engage with the business by offering customers exclusive information, text a request for a call or allow customers to see more information about a product or service.

Audience

If you are going to use QR codes, you need to make sure that your audience are likely to use SmartPhones – and know what to do with a QR code! You will generally be focusing on your customers rather than influencers. You also need to make sure that the landing page works on a SmartPhone!

Time

It takes no longer than 5 minutes to create the QR code and include on promotional material, but you may need to put more time into thinking how you are going to use the QR code to capture email addresses or engage with your audience.

Cost

QR codes are currently free to use. You may need to add an additional landing page to your website.

Measurement

You can identify who clicked through to the landing page on your website or who contacted you using the QR code to text you.

Examples

- Tesco's have a shop in Gatwick airport which is driven by QR codes. Customers scan the QR code of the products they want to buy which are then delivered when they return from holiday.
- A hotel chain has added QR codes to menus in the restaurant. Scanning the QR code will show a video of the dish being prepared by the chef.
- Use QR codes to display a video showing more information about your product or service.
- Use the QR code in the back of this book. In return for your email address, you will entered into a draw to win a 1 hour Skype consultancy call with Mary Thomas. *(One winner every 1 month)*

6.5 LinkedIn

LinkedIn is often the first Social Media site that people are aware of. You may have received invitations to connect from people you know or perhaps people you don't know. LinkedIn is generally considered to be a professional Social Networking site rather than used for personal networking.

By connecting with people on LinkedIn you build an extended contact network. Your extended network gives you access to contacts who are three degrees of separation from you. When you create a LinkedIn profile, you enter business information about yourself and your business. This is often likened to a CV.

I connect on LinkedIn with people I know and would recommend, people who I share many mutual contacts with or people who fall into my potential target groups. I want to be able to use my extended network to provide valuable contacts for myself and others rather than connecting with everybody who asks me.

Why use LinkedIn?

You can use LinkedIn to:

- **Be found by others on LinkedIn**
- **Be found by search engines**
- **Research people and companies**
- **Raise your profile through involvement in group discussions**
- **Publicise events**
- **Talk to your contacts past and present via status updates**
- **Advertise jobs.**
- **Talk to your staff, customers or business partners using a closed group.**
- **Publish a longer form post using LinkedIn publishing**

Audience

Your audience will include people you know or used to know. It will include customers as well as competitors. Your profile will also be seen by people you don't know and by search engines, so do make sure it accurately reflects your brand and values.

Time

Once you have set up your profile (which can take a full day), the main time you will spend is on updating your status, building relationships with others and getting involved in group discussions. I recommend that you update your LinkedIn status and spend time on relationship development most days each week which will take you a minimum of 1 hour a week. However, with LinkedIn, the more time you put in, the more you will get out of it. You can easily spend an hour a week by becoming involved in group discussions.

Be wary of trying to save time by updating one Social Networking tool (say Twitter) and using the same updates on LinkedIn. This can alienate your audience.

For Example

- Joe Bloggs uses LinkedIn and is connected to Tom Smith and Jane Brown
  - Joe has chosen not to use Twitter

- Tom Smith uses LinkedIn and Twitter

- Jane Brown uses LinkedIn and Twitter

- Tom updates his Twitter account several times a day and posts the same updates to LinkedIn

- Jane updates her Twitter account several times a day, but has chosen to only update LinkedIn once a week with a relevant update

- Joe reviews his LinkedIn once a week. He sees updates from Tom, but doesn't understand the Twitter language and the frequency and irrelevance of the updates is annoying. He turns off all updates from Tom. However, he enjoys seeing Jane's update and likes to see how she is getting on, even if the update isn't always directly relevant to him.

LinkedIn Adverts are available for a business and can be targeted by location, age, gender, business role and industry. Advertising on LinkedIn can be quite expensive.

Cost

LinkedIn is a free tool. Although there is a premium option, there is no need for most small and medium sized business owners to upgrade if they have built up a good network of contacts. Therefore the only cost is the time that you and your employees spend using the tool.

Measurement

You can see how many people have looked at your profile and how many times you have appeared in the search results. I find the main measure of success is how many new clients I find as a result of sharing updates, published posts and connecting.

Examples

- An IFA found LinkedIn to be useful to see who his clients were friendly with. By referring to these potential clients by name, he was able to get introductions

- A business consultant was contacted by potential partners because of the information on her LinkedIn profile

- An accountancy firm gained more clients by being part of an extended contact network and letting their contacts know the extent of services they offered

- A firm of solicitors used LinkedIn to build their visibility and reputation

- A trainer got in touch with clients she worked with five years ago, but had lost contact with. Through making contact on LinkedIn, they are now doing business together again

- A discussion in a group led to work and recommendations for me.

6.6 Twitter

Twitter is all about communicating with others in a much more informal and personal way. People choose to follow you (or see your updates) based on the interest of your tweets, the personal connection that they already have with you or because you have been recommended by others. You will be followed by people you don't know. Some of these people will want to get to know you better or find your tweets interesting; there will be some that follow you simply to spam you and you can block them.

Twitter allows you to group people into lists to make it easier to see what people are saying in their status updates. You cannot use Twitter to message only the people in a list. A status update or 'tweet' is up to 140 characters in length and can include links to website pages, photos or documents. There are a variety of Social Media management tools (HootSuite, Tweetdeck, Sproutsocial etc.) which make it easier to listen to your lists of people and engage with them.

Twitter works best if you rethink the way you are marketing. Traditional marketing is much more a 'broadcast' method. Twitter works best if you think about engagement. You need to talk to and reply to people on Twitter, remembering that it is public. Share what other people say and share links to content written by others.

Why Tweet?

Twitter isn't for every business, but some reasons you might want to use Twitter include:

- **Visibility of your product or service**
- **Brand building**
- **Sharing links, updates and information from others**
- **Asking questions and getting information from the Twitter community**
- **To provide customer service**
- **To keep in contact with people you have met face to face**
- **To drive traffic to your website.**

In a tweet you can say anything, but some ideas include:

- **A broadcast of your latest news, offers or events**
- **Information about what you are doing (either personal or business)**
- **A piece of useful information (a tip, a quote)**
- **A link to a useful resource (an interesting article on the internet, your email newsletter)**
- **A reply to somebody else (a conversation)**

- **Forward an interesting tweet to your followers (known as a retweet or RT).**

To me it is very important that you are always positive on Twitter. Twitter is a very public forum and whatever you say will be visible to everybody. It is important that what you say and when you say it reflects your brand and values.

For example, don't use a business account to talk about the latest thing going on in X-Factor – unless this is an important part of your business. Don't use a business account to say that you 'don't have much work and are going back to bed'. You should include some personal tweets though to bring some personality to the business.

Audience

Twitter is public. You may think you are talking to everybody who is following you, but there are ways of listening to what you are saying without publicly following you. Everything that you say can be seen by anybody who looks at your profile.

Time

You should aim for three to five updates each working day. Some of these you can schedule to happen automatically, others will be in real time, such as comments on news or other people's tweets. You need to listen and respond to others on Twitter. I suggest you plan to spend about half an hour a day on Twitter.

Cost

Twitter (at the moment) is a free tool. Some of the management tools have free versions and paid for versions depending on what functionality you require from the tool. There is a time cost though and this shouldn't be underestimated. I would urge you to make sure that Twitter is the right tool for your business before starting. You may want to only 'listen' on Twitter so that you can react if necessary, but not publicise your account.

Measurement

You could measure the amount of followers you have on Twitter, but it is difficult to measure how many of these are appropriate followers. There are tools (including Klout and Kred) that are meant to be able to measure the influence that somebody has, but these tools can be manipulated. The best way of measuring success is by the amount of engagement, Retweets or links through to your website. I also measure success by the number of clients and referrals I have had through Twitter.

Examples

- A firm of accountants have found clients directly through Twitter by responding to people complaining about filling in their VAT return

- Many companies use Twitter to provide customer service. Easy Jet and BT are big companies that successfully provide customer service using Twitter. They realise the importance of addressing any problems promptly

- A restaurant attached to an organic farm has been using Twitter since summer 2009. The owner of the restaurant started by following people on Twitter in the geographical area. His tweets were interesting and largely about the farm. He took the time to converse with the people who started following him. He gained a good reputation and therefore following on Twitter. He then dropped in the odd comment about the restaurant. Over time, people came to the restaurant to try the food and meet the owner in person. In a year this created a large amount of visitors and income for the restaurant.

Don't forget to fill in Exercise 9

6.7 Facebook

Facebook can be used in a number of ways. Many people use Facebook to keep in touch with friends and family as well as colleagues and it is primarily used for status updates, pictures and videos. Although at first glance the information about a person or company is not as extensive as on LinkedIn, the introduction of Facebook Timelines mean that it is very easy to use Facebook to see what somebody posted five years ago.

You need to take care when using Facebook that you set your security options so that you distinguish whether you send status updates to friends or business colleagues. Generally, on Facebook, people only connect with people that they know or have contacts in common with.

Businesses use Facebook to create a business page, which are public and appear in search results.

Why use Facebook?

You can use Facebook at a personal level to keep in contact with friends and family. Some of these Facebook contacts are people that you have met through business and so you can use your personal profile to keep in contact with your business colleagues at a personal level. It is entirely up to you to decide how much personal information you share with others and how wide you set your security settings.

When your business creates a Facebook business page, you can encourage your known and unknown contacts to 'like' the page. When updates are made to your page, these updates appear on the 'news feed' of each of the contacts who like your business page. In reality, it is a little more complicated than that as Facebook has now developed an algorithm to decide which updates appear above others. You need to work quite hard to get your business updates seen.

The other advantage of using Facebook pages is that you can easily share photos and videos with your customers. You can also offer discount vouchers and share information about forthcoming events. In my opinion, Facebook business pages work best for those businesses that have multiple photos or videos to share, as this is the type of information that is 'liked' or 'commented' upon most often. Retail businesses with a target audience of consumers will also find that Facebook business pages work well.

Like LinkedIn, you could use a closed Facebook group to communicate with your staff and allow them to communicate with each other.

Facebook adverts are similar to Google Ads but can be much more targeted. Adverts can be targeted based on the profile information of people you want to reach – location, age, marital status, gender or educational level.

Audience

Your audience for your personal profile will depend on who you have connected with and how you have set your security settings. You can control your own personal profile. A Facebook business page is public and can be seen by all, but no one can see who the administrator behind your Facebook business page is.

Time

You should aim to update your personal Facebook profile several times a day and your business Facebook page at least once a day. Facebook is a tool that needs to be worked at regularly to get results – and the return on investment will depend on your audience groups and type of business. In my opinion, the amount of time that I need to spend to get my business (business to business) seen on Facebook updates is not worth the investment. However I have worked with a number of retail businesses who have seen a great deal of engagement and sales.

Cost

Using Facebook is free, but any adverts will cost if you use them. The main cost of Facebook is time and it is easy to spend too much time on your personal Facebook.

Measurement

Although the number of 'likes' you receive is a measure, the best one is the amount of engagement you get on your Facebook page. Facebook has an extensive suite of tools (Insights) that help you to understand the success of your page and analyse which updates get the most engagement.

Examples

- A business owner has recently started to work with a personal trainer. He decided to create a Facebook page to document his journey. He posted a number of videos of his exercise regime and the advice from his personal trainer. This has resulted in a large number of hits on the videos, and traffic to his business website has increased dramatically. People have got to know him through his videos and now are interested in doing business with him.

- A shopping centre is using Facebook adverts to target people in their geographical area and to update fans on their latest offers and news. Discount vouchers are available for 'one day only' on Facebook. This encourages people to 'like' the page so that they get the offers.

- A drinks company uses Facebook to talk to their fans. They have a knitting charity which they promote on Facebook (raising £200,000 by knitting hats for their drinks bottles) and they promote competitions on the Facebook page. They encourage fans to post photos of the hats they have knitted. One of the great things about this site is that the drinks company comment on each posting and each picture.

- A shoe company used Facebook to build up a fan base, giving out information about their shoes, discounts and offers. They established a good level of engagement with their fans and by analysing the demographics of their fans, they identified a new market opportunity.

6.8 Google+

Google+ is a social network site with similar concepts to Facebook, LinkedIn and Twitter. One of the main differences is that in order to follow somebody you have to immediately put them into a Circle. This is the case for both personal and business Google+ profiles. You can then choose to send an update to one or more of your circles. This means that you can send messages to segments of your audience very effectively. As a business, this is something you cannot do easily in the other tools.

Why use Google+?

As a business, the main reason for using Google+ is that it affects how you appear in search results. Sites on Google+ tend to be indexed very quickly. Those sites with +1 links may be ranked higher in search results.

If you are a local business with a Google Local profile, your Google Local profile is linked to your Google+ profile and people can write reviews and leave tips for others which will affect your ranking in search results. It is also possible to include a 360° photograph of your shop or restaurant in Google+.

Hangouts are a feature of Google which allow you to hold webinars with up to 9 other people for free. You can share screens, watch videos and collaborate on documents. You can live stream the webinar to your video channel on YouTube, your Google+ profile and your website to allow your hangout to be seen by a much larger audience. When the webinar is finished, you can edit and publish the webinar as a standard YouTube video. This is all free of charge. This is a powerful feature that businesses and education will exploit more and more.

You could also use Hangouts to hold free webinars with your staff or business partners.

Another interesting part of Google+ is the way events are promoted with good image design and a link to Google calendar. Reminders are automatically sent to anybody attending the event.

Audience

Google+ has a large number of registered users, but in all honestly not many of them actually directly use the platform to engage. However the tools within Google+ like Hangouts, Local Business integration, communities and links to search means that the audience may be indirect rather than direct.

Time

Time should be spent setting up the Google+ profiles and planning and creating relevant hangouts. Although it is worth using the Posts tool to see if you can reach an appropriate audience, this may be the least effective social networking channel.

Cost

All of the Google+ tools are free. Hangouts may be a low cost way of hosting webinars with your audience.

Measurement

A real measure of the success of Google+ will be how much engagement your business develops and how much time you save by using the Hangouts to market to other businesses. Due to the way that Google search algorithms are changing, it may be necessary, over time, to measure the success of Google+ in the way your website appears in search results. Right now, this is difficult to measure but no doubt will develop.

Examples

- A chef uses Google+ hangouts to broadcast cooking programs.

- A large news organisation uses Google+ to send out relevant content to each of its audience groups

- A company which sells office equipment is considering using Google+ Hangouts to offer educational advice to its VIP customers. Google+ Hangouts are cheaper and easier than using traditional webinar software.

6.9 Podcasts

With the increase in use of Smartphones, podcasts have seen a growth in popularity. Podcasts are an audio file of an interview, magazine style entertainment, radio or TV programme. Businesses can create audio versions of blog entries, interviews with colleagues or expert guests. They can be made available via iTunes or other sharing sites for free or can be bought from the business website.

Why use Podcasts?

It is always a good idea to release your material in a number of different formats. Some people prefer to listen to information than read or watch it. Podcasts are easy to produce using a microphone and a free tool like Audacity. Using voice is a great way of getting your brand and values across; you could even use two voices in the same podcast to simulate a scenario or interview.

Audience

You can make your podcasts available to anybody, but your main audience is likely to be current or future customers.

Time

Once you have the material, it is surprisingly easy to record five to eight minute snippets of information. The material could come from a blog entry or other article you have written.

Cost

It is a good idea to invest in a high quality microphone. The Snowball Blue works well. Other than that, the main cost is your time as there is no cost for Audacity or iTunes. Your website may need to be altered if you want to allow people to buy the podcasts from your site.

Measurement

The best measure of success is the number of downloads of your podcasts, together with comments and general feedback you receive.

Examples

- Leadership and management companies create podcasts to explain their techniques

- Marketing companies create podcasts to give marketing tips and techniques

- An author of a self-improvement book has created a number of podcasts to help sell the book

6.10 Video

YouTube is the second most used search engine. There are YouTube videos available about almost anything. You could also use tools to create short videos to distribute on social media. There are six main types of video:

1 Viral

Videos that appeal to a certain audience who share and promote them with their friends. These videos can generate tens of thousands of views in a very short space of time. In order for a video to become viral it needs to be original, unusual and normally funny and you need to have a certain amount of luck and timing. Viral videos generally generate brand awareness – you need to make sure your brand appears in a positive light!

2 Educational

Educational videos inform people about something that will help them in the future. Typical examples include 'How To' videos that show you, for example how to apply makeup, or use an application. If you create enough educational videos, you can establish trust, credibility and thought leadership. If you inform people for free, they will come to you when they need more information, which they are prepared to pay for.

3 Conversion

Conversion videos are frequently seen on a landing page of a website telling or showing the viewer why they should buy the product or service. The aim of these videos is to keep people engaged and draw them into the site. You will normally have a specific goal in mind, such as encouraging people to leave their email details or buy your product or service. The video should have a clear and demanding call to action.

4 Promotional

Videos of other people giving you testimonials or videos that talk about your business. These videos allow people to get to know the people behind your business. You may want to show videos of your products in use, or what goes on behind the scenes of your business.

5 Live Streaming

We have already discussed the use of Google+ Hangouts. Recently Blab.im has been developed which allows instant public video chat with 4 presenters and an unlimited audience who can comment via text chat. Blab works with a Twitter login and allows the video chat to be recorded.

Other methods of live streaming video include Meerkat and Periscope. These are both apps that run on SmartPhones or tablets and allow users to share where they are, who they are with or what they are doing with visitors who can join the live stream via Twitter. Both Meerkat and Periscope have seen an amazing uptake since they were launched in early 2015. A business could use these live streaming tools to broadcast from events or conferences, hold live Q&A sessions, launch a new product or share a company event. As with all social media, the possibilities are only limited by your creativity.

6 Short

Short videos of 6 seconds (to share on Twitter) or 30 seconds (to share on Facebook) can be created to deliver a specific message. These need to be of high impact and grab a viewer's attention in the first 2 seconds to ensure time is taken to watch them.

The video does not have to be of professional quality; using a High Definition camera with external microphone and tripod will work successfully. Full length videos should be included on YouTube, on your website, in your Facebook and Google+ business profiles and on Vimeo. Even full length videos should be kept to no more than 4 minutes in length, unless there is a compelling reason to make them longer. Short videos can be distributed through social media and included on your website.

Why use Videos?

Videos bring credibility to your product or service and can bring your business to life. They are more accessible than text and offer the viewer interesting information. A video version of your blog (known as a vlog) is a more interactive and animated way of making your content available. You can make the video engaging by asking for comments and responding to any comments you get.

Since YouTube is the second largest search engine, if you tag your video with keywords or phrases it has more chance or being found and watched. If you help people via a video for free with some tips, you build a level of trust and brand awareness. You will need to create a number of videos on your channel to provide credibility.

Audience

Your audience will be your potential customers and people who just want the information, with no intention of becoming your customer. I have a video on YouTube that has been viewed over 19,796 times by people who are unlikely to ever become my customers – they just found that the video answered their question.

Time

Depending on the type of video and the amount of editing you do, it can take anything from half an hour for a 'How To' video of screen shots and speech or a short video capture, to five hours to edit several clips and include music.

Cost

There will be a cost of the video camera (or you can use a Smartphone), the microphone and the tripod, if you use one. For a full length video you are likely to have to pay for video editing software as you will need to add title screens, annotations, call to actions, etc. You could look at Windows Movie Maker, Serif Movie Plus, iMovie and others to edit the video. You might want to do a screen capture using Screencast-O-Matic, Camstudio or Screenr.

Depending where you choose to host your videos, there may be a monetary cost as well as time. It is free to put videos onto YouTube and you can list them as public or 'unlisted'. If you choose to load the videos as 'unlisted', only the people who have the link to the video can view it. Another option is to have a monthly subscription to Amazon S3, which offers a secure hosting service. Reasons for using Amazon S3 over YouTube include: possible security issues, no concern about

the account being closed and having more control over what is seen at the end of the video. Short videos using Vine or Instagram are free to create.

Measurement

There are a number of ways of measuring the success of your videos including number of subscribers to your channel, number of video views, number of comments, at which point during each video people stopped watching and the number of hits on your website from your video channel. In the case of Conversion videos, there should be a direct link between the number of views and the number of conversions.

Examples

1 Viral video
An example is a very successful marketing campaign by the manufacturer of a blender. They shot videos of blending different kitchen and technology items (including an iPhone) to see whether it would blend. The videos are very funny and were spread across the internet by fans. This increased brand recognition and massively increased sales of the blender.

2 Conversion Video
An author got a video made of a review of his book. The video included the reviewer talking about the book as well as screen shots of the book. All the way through the video, the viewer is encouraged to download a free chapter or purchase the entire book.

3 Educational Video
There are many videos available to tell you how to use technology. You can find out 'How To' use all the Social Media channels as well as 'How To' use your iPad or iPhone.

4 Promotional
A company advertising a children's farm made a video of their young lambs. The video was amusing and encouraged people to visit the children's farm at Easter. I have a number of testimonial videos that also serve this purpose.

5 Live Streaming
A number of online clothing companies offer live video as a way of providing customer service.

6 Fashion companies
often use short videos to display their latest styles.

6.11 Images

For some businesses it may make sense to share images relating to your product or business. There are currently two main two channels (other than social networking) for sharing images. Pinterest and Instagram.

6.11.1 Pinterest

Pinterest is a way of sharing and bookmarking images. A business creates a 'board' relating to an area of interest / relevance. The business will pin (bookmark) images to that board. Pinning images from other businesses as well as your own makes the board interesting to more people. Images should be interesting, relevant and where possible, quirky to gain more interest. You can think of Pinterest as an interactive scrap book

Why use Pinterest

Pinterest is a fantastic site for those with a very visual business. If you are not a visual business, you can still use the site for brand awareness by creating boards about an interest relevant to your audience. For example, if you find that a number of your audience have young children, then create a board containing images of things that would be interesting or helpful to this audience. The board will link to your website. If other people repin images from your board, then your brand will get seen by more people. People can comment and like the things that you pin. Just like other Social Networks, people can follow you and your boards.

Pinterest drove three times more referral traffic than Twitter, YouTube, LinkedIn and Google+ combined according to Shareaholic's Quarter 3 2014 report. Monetate reported that the average order value was higher for people who were referred from Pinterest.

Audience

The audience of Pinterest was traditionally female, but that is changing as more and more people enjoy using the visual and creative nature of the tool.

Time

As a business, you need to take time creating boards and collecting content – yours and others. Like many of the other channels discussed in this book, the more effort you put in, the more you will get out of the channel Just make sure the time you are spending on Pinterest is working towards your overall business goals.

Cost

There is no cost on Pinterest, though you may have to pay to have high quality images taken or created of your products and services.

Measure

You can measure the number of followers, repins, comments and likes on any board. Use your analytic tools to see the numbers of clicks to your website.

Examples

- Bottica, an online shop selling jewellery, bags and accessories found that their Pinterest boards resulted in more new users, spending more money than their Facebook Page

- UNICEF created a pinboard for a poor African girl with images for the essentials of life. A million people saw the campaign within a few days.

- Travel companies can use Pinterest to show what is available in the local area. For example, a hotel can use Pinterest to showcase local attractions, walks, venues etc.

6.11.2 Instagram

Instagram is an online photo and video-sharing site that enables its users to take pictures and videos, apply digital filters to them, and share them on a variety of social networking services as well as within Instagram itself.

Why use Instagram?

People can follow each other within Instagram and comment, like and share photos or videos. If you use Instagram you can sync photo or video sharing to other social networks. Using Instagram allows you to create high quality, interesting images to show your products or images related to your business services.

Think outside the immediate services that you provide and think about images or visual content that you can use to engage with your audience. Always answer the question 'So What?'.

Like with any social networking service, you also need to listen to what others are saying and share, comment and like on other people's images.

Audience

You may find a completely different audience on Instagram. The latest figures indicate that 53% of online 18 – 29 year olds and 25% of 30 – 49 year olds use Instagram.

Time

The amount of time you use on Instagram could be minimal if you get into the habit of taking regular images of your products using the Instagram app. It is intended to be quick to use and informal rather than an image designed and crafted over time.

Cost

There is no cost associated with using Instagram though ads are being introduced so this will become a paid option.

Measurement

Instagram provides tools to measure the number of followers and amount of engagement in terms of the number of photos shared, the number of likes and comments they generate and the overall reach of the account.

6.12 Forums

Forums are discussion areas available on internet sites. You can join some forums for free; others have a membership fee. You can include a profile, normally an individual one, ask and answer questions and get involved in discussions.

Why use Forums?

You may want to participate in forums that are applicable to your sector. For example, as an accountant you may want to join Accountancy Age. The advantage of doing this is to get your voice heard within your industry. It may be more worthwhile joining forums that your audience belong to. For example, if you are selling products for children, you may want to consider creating relationships with the people in the Mumsnet forum since this may be where you will find your potential customers.

Be careful not to jump in with a selling message though. Take the time to listen and participate in discussions that are not directly related to your business. Over time people will want to find out more about you and your business.

The other advantage of using forums is to create back links to your website to help to improve your Google rankings.

Audience

In joining a forum you may discover a completely different or new audience of future customers or competitors. Forums are often good ways of making contact with key influencers within the industry or the audience.

Time

You can spend several hours on forums each week, so you need to be very focused on an appropriate small number. You should aim to spend at least one hour a week on your chosen forums.

Cost

Many forums have a membership fee, but some are free. Make sure that if you pay a membership fee, you do get involved in the discussions and complete your profile.

Measurement

Check the analytics of your website to see how many visitors arrive from the forums. Look at the responses to any discussions that you participate in. Measure how many people contact you directly from the forums

Don't forget to fill in Exercise 9

Examples

- **www.4networking.biz** is an online networking forum where you can get business help, provide business solutions and increase your internet presence. There are other similar forums including Women's Business Club, UK Business Forum and UK Business Labs.

- **Quora** is a question and answer site which is being used by many people including those in senior positions in large companies. To use the site, you sign up, ask a question and the question is answered by other users with different experiences. The questions being asked vary from 'What will be the next hot topic in Social Media?' through to 'What factors led to the bursting of the internet bubble in the late 90s?' This second one has been answered by Steve Case, Co-founder of AOL. Quora could be worth a look for two reasons – it is interesting to read some of the answers and answering questions is another way of increasing your personal visibility.

- Reddit is a combination of a forum and a social networking site. Users can share interesting articles, ask questions and share stories. Others vote the updates up or down the site so the most popular are seen by more people. A particularly popular thread on Reddit is AMA (Ask Me Anything). In an AMA, an individual answers any question asked by others on Reddit. The most popular AMA Reddits have featured President Obama and Gordon Ramsey.

6.13 Other Content

As part of a content marketing strategy, you may produce content in other forms including pdf documents, presentations on SlideShare, infographics, e-books or other content that you give away as added value. You should think about a series of content over time rather than one-offs.

Content needs to be professional and add value. You should take the time to write good quality articles / presentations that address people's pain, answer your audience's questions or relate to a current topic of conversation. You must ensure that they contain quality graphics, have been proof read and reflect your brand or values. You may want to give away some content for free with a call to action for additional content in return for an email address. You should create a content strategy so that it is clear what content you are creating and to ensure that each piece of content is created with a specific aim in mind. Each piece of content should have appropriate links to your Social Media profiles, website, etc.

Why Publish Content

Publishing a variety of content increases your internet footprint, makes your brand more visible and adds to your credibility. Your branding will be seen by people in multiple places. Capturing email addresses allows you to build your database and a good follow up strategy ensures you achieve your aims.

Audience

The content should be aimed at a particular audience – customers, influencers, etc. Potentially the content you create will be seen by all of your audience groups. If you include links to share your content on social media sites, it should get seen by more people. Be aware that some media companies look for good quality content to use so this might be a good way of getting found by influencers in your sector.

Time

You will need to allocate time to write the content schedule as well as the time to create the piece of content including graphics, proofreading etc. It will also take time to publish and distribute the content.

Cost

For a fee, you can outsource any of this process. You can pay businesses to write content, create graphics, proofread and distribute the content for you.

Measure

The success of the content you create will be measured by the number of downloads, clicks to the website and shares on Social Media sites. You will need to understand whether the content is the main way people find you or adds to the overall credibility.

Example

- HubSpot sells marketing software. As part of their marketing strategy, they produce vast quantities of useful articles, newsletters, how to guides and eBook downloads. They have a large database and a highly visible brand.

6.14 Social Bookmarking

Social bookmarking sites store links to other sites in a very public way. Links can be images or text and can be tagged with keywords. Other people can find and see your links and bookmark the links if they find them interesting.

You can use social bookmarking sites to store any internet link that you find interesting and would like to store for future use. When you do this, you tag the link with keyword phrases. Other people can search the site on those keyword phrases and may find your link.

On some social bookmarking sites, people can vote on the quality of the links that have been bookmarked. Those links with the most votes will appear higher in search results. Taking this to an extreme, you can build a network of people who have similar interests as you, as people in the network are encouraged to vote on each other's links.

Why use Social Bookmarking?

From a business point of view, you should encourage people to bookmark links from your website and blog. It is also a good idea to bookmark your own links and blog so that the social bookmarking sites know of their existence. The more people who bookmark your links, the more people will see the links and go to your website. The number of bookmarks a link has will also be visible to search engines and may impact on how a search engine ranks your website.

- **Using social bookmarking can be very successful to drive traffic to your website or blog. Some social bookmarking sites allow you to add your blog to the site automatically so each new blog post gets posted.**

Using social bookmarking is also a great method of storing your own interesting links. You can organise your own information in an easy to find way using tags.

Audience

It is a good idea to include share buttons on every link or blog and encourage people to share the content. The audience of the social bookmarking links will be anybody who searches social bookmarking sites for information as well as search engines.

Time

You can include social bookmarking buttons as Add Ins to many Internet browsers and so bookmarking content should simply be a click of a button.

Cost

Social bookmarking sites are free to use. If appropriate for your audience, a small business could spend time establishing a community on Social Bookmarking sites.

Measurement

Using Google Analytics, you can measure which of your website links or blog links come from Social Bookmarking sites. You can also measure where your website is ranked by Google.

Examples

- **Digg** – Submit your blog to Digg and it will get voted upon. A great way to share blog posts

- **Delicious** – Each bookmark can be tagged with your own choice of words. Current trending words are shown on the home page.

- **StumbleUpon** – Displays website pages based on selected topics You can vote ('thumbs up') on websites that you like which will then show you more similar websites. As a business, you can submit (and thumbs up) your own pages and include them in appropriate categories. You can also fill in a profile so people will know who you are when you 'thumbs up' their page.

- Online magazines submit their articles to social bookmarking and encourage their readers to vote for them.

Remember: Don't only bookmark your own sites; bookmark others to share information with other people.

6.15 Mobile Marketing

A 2015 Accenture report found that 87% of consumers use more than one device while watching TV. In fact, there is now a facility for the bigger brands to 'listen' for when an advert is appearing on TV and then automatically reinforce the messages in the advert to people using social media through promoted posts.

Even when people are out and about, many will have access to a mobile device to search for information, find maps, update or check social media, consume music or video, purchase goods, check the news, etc. As a business, you need to consider whether your audience is using mobile devices to look for your products and services and how they are finding the experience.

At the very least, it is becoming essential to have a mobile optimised website. This is a website that either automatically resizes to work on a mobile device or is a separate version of the website that has been written for mobile devices. It is essential not only because you want your visitors to be able to have a good interaction with your site irrelevant of the device they are using, but also early in 2015, Google changed its mobile search algorithm to prioritise mobile optimised sites.

In general, whenever using social media to communicate with your audience, you need to remember that they may be viewing the information on a mobile device so you need to think about how the images will look on mobile. These days, most of the sites will resize images automatically – but it is also worth checking yourself (on a variety of devices) whether your content is appearing correctly.

There are a number of other methods of mobile marketing you may wish to explore:

Text message SMS Marketing

An efficient and cost effective way of delivering information to a targeted group of customers. According to one source, 95% of SMS messages are open and read within 3 minutes.

Mobile Apps

If a customer wants to engage more with a business, they may download a mobile app. An app can provide a value added service with targeted information. A business may want to consider developing an app as a loyalty card (Gourmet Burger Kitchen), a shopping service (Argos) or a source of information (BBC). The car parking service Apcoa has an app which identifies which car park you have arrived at and makes the process of paying for a ticket quick and straightforward.

Near Field Communication or Blue Tooth Beacons

This is technology that works when customer are located near to a business. Information about the business or special offers available can be sent directly to mobile devices. Facebook are distributing bluetooth beacons to local businesses in the US to help people see more about the business when they visit.

The use of mobiles is only increasing and it is important when creating your strategy that you consider whether your audience is going to be searching for your products and services using a mobile device. If they don't immediately have a good experience when they have found your products and services, your prospect will quickly move on.

6.16 Digital Advertising

In the UK, advertisers spent £3.98 billion on digital advertising in the first half of 2014 (up 13.4% year on year). The advantage of digital advertising is that it can be highly targeted and low cost. For example, a Facebook advert can be targeted by location, gender, age, household composition, marital status, household income, interests, and digital activity. The advert can be charged at pay per click or pay per impression and can cost as little as £0.20 / click (for adverts that get lots of engagement). The return on investment can be massive.

It is important however that there is a clear reason or aim for the advert. The aim of the advert should be linked to the overall marketing objectives, have a specific target audience and have measurable outcomes. You should understand the response you require from the advert.

- If you want the advert to drive traffic to your website, there should be a focused landing page with a clear call to action to tell the customer what to do next – sign up for a webinar, download a document, trial a product, etc. – where possible you should aim to get the customer's email address so you can follow up the marketing message.

- You may want the customer to call you or chat to you using webchat. Again, the advert should direct customers to a landing page with clear information about what to do next. If they do use the webchat or pick up the phone, ensure that the person answering knows what the intended outcome is and how to move the prospect towards the intended outcome – and of course, make sure there are enough people available to answer.

- If you want to increase followers or fans – make sure you are targeting the ad at a relevant audience who will want to talk to you in the future and tell them why they should follow your page – what is in it for them.

- You may wish to run a digital advertising campaign to purchase something either online or offline using a coupon code. Again, make sure the coupon code is easy to use and remember. When customers click the ad they must be taken to a place on your website where they can use it or receive information about their nearest store.

The other important thing to consider when running a digital advert is the importance of the image. The best images are ones that are eye catching, different and aspirational. You want your audience to want to connect with the image and be involved with the campaign. Do experiment with different images and different messages, we have found that our audience do not always connect with the image we expected them to.

When you are running a digital advertisement campaign, it is important to track and measure its success. Sometimes a small change can make a huge difference to the numbers of people who engage with the advert. It is also always important to track what you are spending against what you are receiving in increased subscribers or revenue to ensure that the advert is achieving its aims.

Exercise 9: How Am I Planning to Use Each Channel?

	Blogs	Newsletter	FourSquare	Digital Vouchers	QR Codes
I will use short term					
I can see a long term use					
Time I am going to allocate					
Money I am going to allocate					
My reasons for using are					
My audience is					
I am going to talk about					
I am going to measure					
More information, training or people needed					

Exercise 9: How Am I Planning to Use Each Channel?

	LinkedIn	Twitter	Facebook	Google+	Video
I will use short term					
I can see a long term use					
Time I am going to allocate					
Money I am going to allocate					
My reasons for using are					
My audience is					
I am going to talk about					
I am going to measure					
More information, training or people needed					

Exercise 9: How Am I Planning to Use Each Channel?

	Podcast	Images	Forums	Other Content (what?)	Social Bookmarking (which?)
I will use short term					
I can see a long term use					
Time I am going to allocate					
Money I am going to allocate					
My reasons for using are					
My audience is					
I am going to talk about					
I am going to measure					
More information, training or people needed					

6.17 Review of Chapter 6

In this chapter, we have looked at a number of Social Media channels and thought about why you might want to use them, how much time it will take and how you will measure success. Hopefully you have filled in the tables in Exercise 9. Now, take a few minutes to look back at the table. How many boxes have ticks in the "I will use Short Term" row? Is this realistic? Take some time to review the set of tables as a whole.

During the next few chapters we will look at what you are going to say using the channels and the resources you have to use the channels. We will also look at how you are going to measure success and how you are going to set targets against each of the aims you identified in Chapter 3. Finally we will assist you to create a Social Media Strategy.

7.1 Costs and Time

As we identified in Chapter 2, there is a cost associated with all the marketing that you do as a business. This cost may be in terms of time – how long does it take you to attend a networking lunch, including travel time and

to manage that time in-house, while other people outsource their Social Media content to a dedicated Social Media manager, who manages a number of Social Media accounts. There are advantages and disadvantages of each method.

The method you use for your Social Media

In-house Social Media Content Management	Outsourced Social Media Content Management
Can add personality to updates	Constant presence on Social Media without you needing to spend your time
Can respond quickly to messages and trends	Can email or contact your business if necessary
Results of listening can inform business decisions	Reliant on content from your business
Updates show brand and values of business	Profiles set up to represent your business brand
Time cost	Tends to be 'broadcast mode' and less personal
	Financial cost

time at the event? There may be a financial cost – how much does it cost to join the networking group, pay for each lunch and pay for the petrol to get there each month? If your marketing includes promotional material, how much does it cost to design, print and perhaps, deliver the material?

The biggest cost associated with Social Media is that of time. Most of the channels are free to use but there may be a financial cost of training required. Social Media does take time though and there is a financial cost associated with time. Depending on the size of your business and the amount of interaction you have with your customers, the time you need to spend on Social Media will vary. Some larger businesses have an entire department devoted to managing their Social Media. Smaller businesses may try

will depend on a number of factors and below I have listed four options, in order of what I think would work best from a Social Media viewpoint. However, you need to consider your own situation in terms of aims, resources available (time and financial), audience and channels .

1 All areas of your business and people within it, should take responsibility for updating Social Media. This means you need appropriate training and policies and guidelines to be in place.

2 One person in your business takes responsibility for Social Media. This may well be up to 25% of their role depending on the channels you decide to use. Other areas in the business should provide content to be used.

3 A combination of outsourced and internal Social Media. Content can be given to the outsourced resource to schedule; keywords can be identified for analysis and reporting purposes. One person in your business can also update Social Media (say 5% - 10% of their role) giving real time updates, answering questions, commenting as necessary and showing some personality.

4 Outsource all your Social Media. You will need to give content to your outsourced resource who will take care of all the replies, real time updates and engagement. They can provide reports as you require them.

See the chart below for a rough guide of the time you should aim to spend on each Social Media tool. This does not include the time to set up your profiles. Remember, you are unlikely to use every tool!

	Per Month	Per Fortnight	Per Week	Per Day
Blogs			2 hours	
Newsletter	4 – 8 hours			
Foursquare				Monitor
Groupon	Time for a campaign			
QR Codes	1 hour			
LinkedIn				30 minutes
Twitter				30 minutes
Facebook				30 minutes
Google+				30 minutes
Video		5 hours		
Podcast			30 minutes	
Forums			30 minutes	
Other Content	16 hours			
Social Bookmarking			30 minutes	

7.2 Policies and Guidelines

The purpose of a Social Media Policy is to make it clear to your employees what they can and can't do on Social Media and any potential consequences, if appropriate. Each business will have a different Social Media Policy according to their needs. I recommend that all stakeholders are consulted when creating your Social Media Policy. Even if you are a small business, it is a good idea to have a policy so you are forced to think through some of the issues. Make sure it is included in your employee handbook and is given to and understood by all your employees.

Your Social Media Policy should include the following:

1. Why your business is using Social Media – your overall aims

2. What audience you are targeting

3. Your brand and values and how these are represented in Social Media. How are you using Social Media to add value to your audience?

4. How copyright and Intellectual Property Rights (IPR) issues should be handled with respect to Social Media. What needs to remain confidential?

5. How your employees are able to use the Social Media channels. A good rule of thumb is if the employee is not prepared to say something to a client or the Director of the business, they shouldn't say it on Social Media. You may want to include suggestions of content that is and is not acceptable. Include details of how much time your employees can spend on Social Media and whether or not they are allowed to use Social Media for personal use during work time. Identify any potential issues with who your employees can connect to. For example should swimming teachers be allowed to connect to their pupils?

6. If employees want to use Social Media channels to offer a personal opinion, they should include a disclosure along the lines of "The views expressed here are mine and do not represent the views of my employer".

7 If one of your employees is asked to create Social Media profiles and uses them to market your business, your policy needs to detail who owns the channels when the employee leaves the business, to make sure you still have access to the channels.

8 How your reputation is handled on Social Media. This includes who is responsible for monitoring the channels and the chain of command for notification of problems, along with how frequently the channels are monitored.

9 How you handle inappropriate comments by your employees on personal Social Media accounts. You need a link to employment conditions and be specific about consequences if any. You may need to be quite specific about what employees are not allowed to share online.

Once you have decided which employees are going to use Social Media to market your business, you need to make sure that the appropriate training is carried out to ensure they can carry out your Social Media strategy. You may also find a need to educate a wider range of your employees to ensure that when they use Social Media for personal use, they have a clear understanding of the potential consequences for your business. Many people do not understand the public nature of the tools and the impact of saying, "Another boring day at Company X". Spending some time on education now may save you time and money later.

CHAPTER EIGHT

We have identified your aims for Social Media and you have some idea of the channels that you want to use to achieve these aims, as well as the resources that you have to work with. You may be formulating an idea of what you are going to say on Social Media. In this chapter, you will get some ideas for content.

At all times think "add value". You want to give people a reason to follow your updates and be interested in what you have to say. You can add value yourself by talking about something interesting to your audience, or you can add value by sharing what others say. Remember that people love to be stroked – how good does it feel if your update is 'liked', 'shared' or commented upon? Keep it realistic though – if you comment on every update, you will soon devalue the effect.

Your updates should reflect your brand and the values of your business. We discussed brand and values way back in Chapter 2 – you should review the values that you identified in Exercise 1. You need to make sure that your values are reflected in all of the updates that you publish.

For example, I will not use bad language on Social Media channels or post updates outside office hours. If I wanted to 'tweet' about the latest 'The Voice' contestant, I would create a personal profile which was not linked to my business. Similarly, I will not be negative on Social Media as this does not reflect my business values.

Once you start to use Social Media, it is important to continue to have a presence on the channels. One of the ways to do this is to schedule content in advance. This allows you to have a presence without actually doing it in real time. There are channels available to help you to schedule updates on Twitter, Facebook, LinkedIn and Google+. You can also schedule the release of Email newsletters and Blog entries. Be careful though not to just schedule updates. You must also monitor your updates and engage with other people on Social Media. I suggest you put aside time each day, whenever possible to engage in real time conversations with your audience.

In Exercise 10, you will find a list of content ideas you might want to talk about. Have a look at the list and tick which content ideas you want to include, which channels will be most appropriate and what can be scheduled.

Whether you choose to schedule updates or not, I suggest you set up a content calendar. Take the next three to six months and identify what you are going to talk about using each of the channels each month and then each week. The calendar may change as news and real time developments occur. However, at least you have this as a backup and you can prepare blogs and updates ahead of time. There is nothing worse than sitting down to write a blog entry with a blank piece of paper! It takes more time and may end up being less relevant to your audience. The other advantage of creating a content calendar is that other people will be able to implement your Social Media for you.

Exercise 10: Content Ideas

Content	I Will Use	Channel(s)	Schedule?
Add value, give people a reason to follow you			
Give people tips that are relevant to your product or service			
Give answers to questions you are frequently asked about your product or service			
Promote events that you are attending, have attended or are presenting or exhibiting at			
Ask people their opinion of a topical subject			
Give ideas of questions that people should ask if they are going to buy your type of product or service			
Celebrate your successes, keeping client confidentiality, if necessary			
Ask for help in finding a supplier or solving a problem			
Link to or comment on interesting news items			
Share articles that you have read that are related to your product or service			
Personal, real time information			
Reply to other people's comments			
Details of new products or promotions that you are selling (be careful not to overdo this)			
Discounts or coupon codes			
Blogs, articles or presentations that you have written			
News about your company			
Question and Answer session - 'ask an expert'			
Personality of the business - behind the scenes information			
Ask for photos, comments or challenges from your audience			

CHAPTER NINE

In this chapter we bring together the objectives for using Social Media that you identified back in Chapter 3, with the channels and measures of success you identified in Chapter 6.

Measuring the success or return on investment (ROI) of Social Media is important, but still an unknown entity compared to traditional marketing. When measuring the success of a website, analytical tools exist to show hits on the website, bounce rate and time spent on the site. You can identify how many sales you get from people who found you through your website. Similarly when you do a leaflet drop, you can use specific telephone numbers to identify who has contacted you as a result of that particular leaflet drop.

Depending on your objectives for using Social Media and the channels that you use, the return on investment can be measured in several ways. For each objective, you should set SMART targets so that you have some way of monitoring success, otherwise you could spend a great deal of time and money without understanding what (if anything) you are achieving.

SMART stands for Specific, Measurable, Achievable, Realistic and Timely. The idea is that there is little point in setting a target that doesn't conform to these ideals since you are just setting yourself up for failure. You need to make sure that you have identified a realistic numerical target in a given timeframe for each of your Social Media objectives. You may think that it is not possible to measure a target of brand building or building a reputation. A potential

SMART target for this would be "to achieve five recommendations through Social Media in the next six months". You may find that your objectives are met by using several different tools.

Typical ways of measuring success could be an increase, by a certain amount, in a certain timeframe, in one or more of the following:

- **Visits to your website or blog**
- **Comments on your blog**
- **Retweeting of your tweets**
- **Facebook friends, 'likes' or comments**
- **Twitter followers**
- **People who view your LinkedIn profile**
- **Comments on your LinkedIn group discussions or questions**
- **Hits on your videos**
- **Social bookmarking votes**
- **Podcast downloads**
- **Recognition at face to face networking based on your online activity**
- **New business directly through Social Media**
- **Referrals through Social Media.**

In general, you should expect to spend three to six months actively using Social Media before you can decide whether the various channels are working for you. You should spend time listening via the various channels and responding and talking where and when appropriate. I recommend you focus on engagement, mentions and referrals rather than 'followers' or 'likes'.

Over the three to six month period, you should analyse which channels bring you the most engagement and meet the targets you have set for your objectives. You should try a variety of different updates and analyse which bring the most success.

Over time, you need to regularly review your objectives and your Social Media channels to identify what is working and what needs to be changed. You may need to change your content or channels, the way you use a channel, or you may need to engage with a different audience.

Now, complete Exercise 11 to identify SMART targets for each of your objectives that you identified in Exercise 5.

Exercise 11: Measurement

1 **Review each of the objectives that you identified in Exercise 5. You may want to make some changes based on what you have now learnt**

2 **For each objective, identify which Social Media tool or tools you are going to use to achieve it. Write this information down in the table on the next page**

3 **For each objective and channel, set SMART targets you want to achieve.**

Exercise 11: How are you going to measure success?

Objective	Channel(s) To Use	Measure Of Success				
		Specific (What)	Measurable (How Many)	Achievable (How)	Realistic (By Whom)	Timely (By When)

There are a number of tools available to help you measure your rate of success, some paid for and some free. You need to pick the best tool for the size of your business and the amount of information you require.

Free tools for measuring Social Media

These tools will change, appear and disappear over time, but this is a good list to start with. Each tool has advantages and disadvantages and you need to find the ones that work best for your business. Many of these free tools have paid for options which give you more information.

- **Social Mention**
- **Samepoint**
- **HowSocialable**
- **Topsy**
- **Twittergrader**
- **Klout**
- **Kred**
- **Twitterfall**
- **Google Blog search**
- **Boardreader**
- **Quarkbase**
- **HootSuite**
- **Tweetdeck.**

Paid for tools for measuring Social Media

In a larger business you will find you need to use the functionality available in these paid for tools.

- **Radian6**
- **Brandseye**
- **Brandwatch**
- **HootSuite**
- **Tweetdeck**
- **SproutSocial.**

CHAPTER TEN

You started this workbook by reviewing your current marketing and deciding why you wanted to use Social Media.

You then identified your audience groups and looked at the resources you have available. You reviewed each of the available Social Media channels and pinpointed which you are going to use now and which you are going to revisit in the long term. You considered what you are going to say on Social Media and how you are going to measure your efforts. By working through the workbook, you may also have identified some other action points you need to address.

Now you have almost completed the workbook, it is worth spending time going back through the exercises to see if anything has changed.

The final exercise looks forward and helps you to create your Social Media Strategy.

Exercise 12: Social Media Strategy

To complete Exercise 12, pull in information that we have covered earlier in the book. When you look back over the previous exercises, review the information in light of everything you have learnt, rather than just using it word for word.

Social Media Objectives

Exercise 12: Social Media Strategy

Who Should Use Social Media?		
Resource	Training Need	Time

Social Media Channels To Be Used In Next 3 Months		
Channel	Audience	Measurement of Success

Exercise 12: Social Media Strategy

What Should We Talk About?	
Content	Frequency

Other Action Points		
	Person Responsible	By When
Develop Content Strategy		
Develop Social Media Policy and Guidelines		
Training Needs		

CHAPTER ELEVEN

In summary, Social Media is here to stay as a method of promotion. You can choose to take advantage of the opportunity to control your own message or not. If you decide to use it, it is worth investing some time in making sure you exploit the opportunities that Social Media gives.

It is a changing environment though and I suggest that you review your Social Media Strategy every three to six months to make sure that you are using the newest opportunities in the best way for your business.

Here are some final Dos and Don'ts to remember:

Do

- Add value
- Share, 'like' and comment on other people's updates
- Show your personality
- Respond to people who 'like', share or comment on your updates
- Think about your brand and values
- Plan who to talk to and what to talk about
- Continue once you have started
- Get your profiles completed
- Feed information you find out about people into a Customer Relationship Management System
- Understand and find your voice
- Listen to others.

Don't

- Be too personal – telling people about your cup of coffee is not very interesting
- Sell too often (one update in every five is a good rule of thumb)
- Expect too much, too soon
- Be negative about other people or businesses.

And so finally ...

Enjoy developing and using your Social Media Strategy.

Please do connect with me on Twitter @concisetraining or follow Concise Training on LinkedIn or Facebook.

I look forward to hearing from you and would love to hear how you are getting on with your Social Media Marketing.

What Next?

- **I have a strategy – now what?**
- **Where do I start with all these channels?**
- **I need some training!**

Win 1 hour consultancy with Mary Thomas

I hear these comments frequently from business owners and marketing managers I work with; and you may be the same. You can see the need for Social Media Marketing and now you have a strategy, but you don't know where to start with the channels.

You need to learn how to use the available range of Social Media channels. You need to understand how to connect with people, how to create your profile and what to say using the channels, so you don't give the wrong impression about your business!

At Concise Training we can help you learn how to use the channels in a time efficient and cost effective way. We offer a number of approaches depending on how you and your colleagues learn best:

- **Bespoke training courses at your office or over the internet. Training covers what you need to know in a patient, personal and informative way.**
- **Social Media E-Learning courses. Learn how to use the Social Media channels covered in this book in the comfort of your own office at your pace. Our interactive, detailed courses cover 'how to' and 'best practice'.**

- **City & Guilds qualifications in Social Media to kick start your career in Social Media.**

To make the most of your Social Media Strategy and to learn how to put it into practice, get in touch to discuss the training needs of you and your organisation.

"I started the ITQ Social Media qualification with Concise Training and within three months was reaping the rewards! Having completed the qualification successfully, my business has never looked back and we have paid for the training at least eight times over already in revenue generated on the back of it."

Caroline Anderson from Business Boots, Social Media Champion for Small to Medium-sized businesses

Call: 01865 522658

Email: mary@concisetraining.net

Website: www.concisetraining.net